On Eagles' Wings

AN UNTOLD STORY OF THE MAGIC CARPET

I bare you on eagles' wings,
and brought you unto myself.
Exodus 19:4

Captain Elgen M. Long

On Eagles' Wings

AN UNTOLD STORY OF THE MAGIC CARPET

Captain Elgen M. Long

©2016

Printed in the USA

ISBN 13: 978-1523651856
ISBN 10: 1523651857

Book Design, Graphics and Layout
Sigrid K. Powell

Table of Contents

This book is dedicated to the 51,000 Jewish Yemenites who made their Aliyah to Israel on the "Magic Carpet," and to those hundreds of people and organizations who supplied the knowledge, funds, and talent to bring the operation to its complete fulfillment.

Prologue

ON EAGLES' WINGS

This book is dedicated to the heritage of hundreds of thousands of Yemenite Jews whose interesting history stands out in the story of mankind over the last several thousand years.

It is written to relate to those of Jewish heritage from Yemen an untold story of how some of their recent ancestors were brought on emergency flights from Aden to Israel "On Eagles' Wings" in early 1949. This was before Camp Hashed was built or "Operation Magic Carpet" began.

After WW II ended there were millions of Jews dislocated throughout many parts of the world. Their stories of survival and dreams of someday living in a Jewish State are as real and exemplary as the story of the Yemenites. Happenstance put our Alaska Airlines crew in Aden, Yemen, and involved us with the plight of the Jewish Yemenite refugees. The war time secrecy required during the Arab-Israeli War left this story of the Yemenites' early rescue operations untold, and is being revealed for the first time in this book.

While the stalwart Jewish Yemenites are the central heroes of these events, many individuals and governments played significant roles in making it possible. Israeli, British, and United States interests, all made difficult humanitarian efforts in secrecy, during a time of war, to rescue the stranded Jewish Yemenite refugees and fly them to Israel

Enough aviation and governmental details have been included in the writing so aviation interests and historians will be able to have detailed knowledge of the previously undisclosed events that are herein recorded for the first time.

The events I am writing about occurred in 1948 and 1949, over 65 years ago. Most of the participants are no longer with us, and most of our work was done in the shadow of the Arab-Israeli War, when secrecy prevailed. I have had to depend on personal log books, research, my memory, and the recorded memories of others who participated. I hope together they have allowed me to relate the story of the following events in a reasonably accurate manner. If an error in a date, time, event, or person is found in the text I apologize in advance.

During World War II, from 1939 to 1945, it has been estimated over 20 million people died, and tens-of-millions more became refugees who were forced to flee to any place of safety in the world they could reach. While those six years were a dark period in the recorded history of man it was not the only, or the darkest, of many such events.

But this book is not about WW II or a dark period in the history of man. It is about a stalwart people who survived WW II and the nearly 2,000 years preceding it, waiting in a foreign land for the time of their prophesied return to their native land of Canaan. It is a story of faith, and dreams that came true for the Jewish citizens of what, in modern times, has come to be called Yemen.

Recorded history and archeological study have not been able to reveal exactly when or why the Jewish people first settled in the southwestern part of the Arabian Peninsula. While writing this book, for simplification, we will use the area's current name Yemen, and identify the Jewish families that lived there as Yemenite Jews.

There are legends of how the Jewish families' ancestors came to be in Yemen, but the actual history is vague. Written records do indicate an in-migration to south Arabia during the Jewish diaspora around 65 A.D. Though vague, history does confirm that the majority of Jewish families had made their migration to the area before the year 200 AD.

The amazing thing is that during all the nearly 2000 years the Jewish population was isolated in the Southern Arabian Peninsula, they were able to maintain their language and religious beliefs completely intact through to the twentieth century.

Except for a few difficult periods of time when they suffered on-and-off pogroms after the Muslim and Ottomans began trading off ruling dominance, the Jewish citizens were a successful and welcome part of the southern Arabian society.

In more recent years, drought reduced the agricultural production in Yemen, and the country became relatively poor. Regardless, throughout the centuries the Jewish population in Yemen held tightly to their language, culture, and religion. Perhaps what helped them remain so steadfast was the prophecy of "Redemption," recorded in the "Jewish holy book," that one day they were destined to return to the land of Israel and become part of a great and prosperous Jewish Nation.

As your author is not Jewish, and the reader may also not be Jewish, I will use the term "Jewish holy book" when referring to the "Torah," "Prophets," or "Writings" which comprise in sequence the Tanakh.

For simplification, all the Biblical Quotes in the book are taken from the Old Testament of the King James Version of the Bible, and I have used the modern geographical names of places instead of their ancient ones.

Also as I have been an airman for over 70 years, I will occasionally use aeronautical terms and phrases that are antiquated if not completely out dated. In those cases, I will try to make a short explanation of what the term meant at the time.

After WW II Alaska Airlines president James A. Wooten foresaw that there would be a great need and demand for new international charter air services throughout the world. The United States international scheduled airlines were concentrating on developing premier scheduled passenger services between the major cities of the world, while paying little attention to the new freight and low cost utility passenger charter services that were in increasing demand.

These new nonscheduled world charter flights would require new services to be available at airports all over the world to accommodate the non-scheduled charter aircraft that landed there. Alaska Airlines management had the foresight to arrange in advance for contracts with aviation fuel providers world-wide, and a network of handling agents that could coordinate and provide for the nonscheduled charter flights local service needs at major international airports.

On the following pages, I will relate to you the untold story of how five young men, while working for Alaska Airlines in March of 1949, played a crucial role in the making of the nearly 2000-year-old dream of Yemenite Jews come to reality.

While flying refugees during the Arab-Israeli War, our five young men were suddenly confronted with refugee passengers that were faced with a life and death situation. Together, they developed a practical way to overcome the emergency. The procedure they developed with the British Commander at Khormaksar RAF (Royal Air Force) Station in early 1949, proved to be so successful that it has been used over and over again, and is still in use to this day. This is just one of the many adventures recounted on the following pages.

Read, enjoy and learn, as I relive with you in print an untold story of the miraculous return of the Jewish Yemenite refugees to the "Promised Land" of Israel.

Bab Al, Main Entrance Gate to Yemen's Capital City of Sanaa.
From the blog of Francis Mulcahy at www.yobserver.com

Chapter One

THE JEWISH FAMILIES IN YEMEN

And it shall be said in that day,
Lo, this is our God; we have waited for him,
and he will save us: this is the LORD; we have waited for him,
we will be glad and rejoice in His salvation.

Isaiah 25:9

The sun had set behind the nearby hills and the streets and houses of Sanaa, Yemen, and it slowly darkened as it continued its' descent further below the horizon.

Jewish families had lived in Sanaa longer than recorded history and much longer than anyone could remember. In the 20th century, while many Jewish families lived in the heavily populated capital of Yemen, Sanaa, thousands of other Jewish families lived in other cities, towns, villages, and remote areas throughout Yemen. Folklore held that they were descendants of Jewish merchants who had come to Yemen from the Biblical lands of the eastern Mediterranean thousands of years ago. During the passing of those millenia, there were times when the Jews in Yemen had existed as valuable and respected citizens, and at other times held as uncouth infidels, and degraded to second-class citizenship.

The majority of the Jewish families in Yemen had arrived by the end of the 2nd century A.D. and prospered and enjoyed the respect of their Arab neighbors until approximately 800 A.D. It was around that time that the Muslim faith had been introduced by Mohammed into the Arab population on the Arabian Peninsula. Though the Arabs of Yemen embraced the teachings of Mohammed, the Yemenite Jews, generation after generation, continued to adhere to the teachings of the Jewish holy book that their ancestors had meticulously copied by hand. Through the centuries the copies of the Jewish holy book had become their most valuable possession. From the time of their arrival in Yemen, century after century, regardless of the circumstances of their lives, those never changing hand copied scriptures helped the Jewish Yemenite families keep their language, customs, and religious beliefs intact. During most of those centuries, the Jewish

1

families had maintained satisfactory relationships with the Arab majority that was in power. Their skills as silversmiths, craftsmen, farmers, and entrepreneurs were considered essential and necessary by the Arabs. The Yemeni Jewish families had lived an unsophisticated lifestyle, and over a period of nearly twenty centuries and a hundred generations, their culture and beliefs had survived unchanged. Nothing else controlled by humans that I can think of has remained unchanged in this world for such a long period of time.

The world outside of Yemen had gone through the crusades, religious reformations, the middle-ages, the discoveries of other people and continents, and the industrial age. During those centuries the nations of the world and their populations had advanced along with the discoveries of science, industries, and agriculture. By the twentieth-century, steam ships, electricity, sewers, running water, furniture, radios, tractors, automobiles, trains, and airplanes were common throughout the developed world. However, in Yemen, most Jewish families had never seen an airplane, listened to a radio, ridden in an automobile, or had electricity, water, sewer services, or furniture in their homes.

Over generations, the Jewish families had become used to their medieval style of life. To people in the western world, their homes and living conditions would be considered no better than existing in abject poverty in a slum. Few Jews were able to attend schools or receive an education in regular schools, and the children had to depend on their parents and their Rabbi to provide for their scholastic needs. However, to the Jews in Yemen there was something more important to them; they lived by the laws written in the Jewish holy book, and their religious faith in its writings. It was prophesized in the Jewish holy book that there would come a day of redemption. They were destined to make Aliyah, and return to the promised land of Israel to build a great and prosperous nation.

The Hebrew word "Aliyah" in English, can be defined as "ascent," or "progressing towards Jerusalem."

Beginning about the 8th century A.D., Muslims began imposing pressure on the Yemenite Christians and Jews to convert to the Islamic faith. This manifested itself in the application of extra taxes, restrictive laws, and demeaning rules over the non-Muslim citizens. Through the centuries, the Jewish population was able to survive during this period of Muslim theocracy, in part because of the special skills and craftsmanship they possessed that were generally not available or practiced by the Muslim citizens of Yemen.

Yemen's main seaport, Aden, was conquered by the Ottoman Empire in 1548, and Yemen came under Ottoman rule. Though they were also a Muslim country, the Ottoman Empire's rule was not as oriented towards the conversion of

2

its non-Muslim citizens. Over the next 374 years, under the rule of the Ottoman Empire, the theocratic laws were slowly relaxed. This continued until the mid-1850's, when the Ottoman Empire's Grand National Assembly actually switched the Empire from religious law to secular law, making all citizens equal regardless of their religion. As difficult as it had been during those years, the Jews living in south Arabia were still able to keep their language, customs, and religion intact.

In 1922, the Ottoman empire was divided up and made into several different countries and mandates. Yemen became a country that was again ruled strictly by Muslims, and many of the old Muslim theocratic rules returned. Yemenite Jews were again declared to be impure, had to obey subservient and demeaning laws, as well as pay a special tax before they could practice their religion.

After World War II, the typical Jewish family lived in the old section of a city, town, or village. They had no electricity, running water or sewage service in their homes, and the floors were dirt that they covered with hand-made rugs, mats, or mattresses. Furniture, chairs, tables, and bedsteads, as modern citizens in developed nations have, did not exist in their homes. They sat, ate, and slept on the floor. Everyday all the water used in their home had to be carried by the mother and her children from the community water-well. In recent years the Jewish families had been reduced by circumstance and the ruling Muslim Imam Yahya, to living in a state of poverty that only increased their longing for the promised time of redemption.

After the family had completed dinner, the mother and the children would make themselves comfortable, while they listened as their father told them of the day's happenings. The children sat quietly watching their father in the candlelight as he recited the events of the day and outlined what could be expected tomorrow. The father was not just the breadwinner and protector of the family, but because only the wealthy Muslim families had access to schools for their children, he shared with their mother and their rabbi, the responsibility of educating his children.

Their rabbi held religious classes for the children at the synagogue, and they were taught Arabic and how to read and write. They also learned the Jewish customs, writings, prohibitions, and requirements of the Jewish holy book in leading a Jewish life. Many had memorized the religious scriptures and would recite portions of them from memory on the Sabbath meetings that were held every Saturday. The only other substitute for the absence of a regular school curriculum was what the children learned from their parents, relatives, and friends. This was how they had been able to preserve their particular language, culture, customs, and religious beliefs. Many modern linguists believe the particular Hebrew dialect used in Yemen may be the closest, in use today, to the language actually used in Canaan during the time when the Jewish Holy Book was written.

They knew they were Jews, and were being forced to live as second-class citizens in a Muslim country under Muslim rule. Their rabbi and their father had reminded the family many times of the prophecy of the Great Redemption that their scriptures described. The promise of a better future was what sustained them as a people regardless of the circumstances they faced at that moment. Their firm belief in the efficacy of the Jewish holy books' prophecies through the centuries had enabled them to become a courageous people.

A Jewish friend heard in 1948 that there had been declared a Jewish State of Israel, and King David again ruled the land. That wasn't completely correct, though the Jewish State of Israel had been declared, it wasn't King David that ruled, it was Prime Minister David Ben-Gurion.

Also in 1948, after ruling Yemen for 44 years, Imam Yahya was killed and replaced by his son Ahmad.

The head Jewish rabbi for the Yemenites was, Rabbi Levy, and his synagogue was in Sanaa. As he was located in the capital of Yemen he could hear information circulating that those in distant towns and cities were not privy to. To keep the Jewish population informed, Rabbi Levy would spread the information by word of mouth and letters to the Rabbinate of Yemen for dissemination on the Sabbath in the synagogues.

As more bits of information filtered in, the people became more excited, but at the Jewish community meetings on Saturdays, their local rabbi would caution the people to be careful about the possible coming of the time of Redemption. They would be reminded of the false prophets in the past that had come and gone declaring that the time of the Great Redemption had arrived. There were reports that the Arab Muslims were fighting the establishment of the Jewish State of Israel, and they were living in a Muslim country. The advice was to carefully wait for more information, and see what happens before taking any further action.

In the meantime, the Jewish families in Yemen were cautioned by their rabbi to be especially careful when it came to protecting their family. While they waited for confirming information about the possible time of Redemption, they should work at their jobs to be able to continue to supply their families with their needs, while putting a little extra away for the time when the Redemption might actually arrive.

Again, the families were cautioned not to break any of the Muslim Imam's dictates. They were reminded that, because the Muslims considered the Yemeni Jews impure, they were not to touch a Muslim or any of their food. If a Muslim attacked them they must not strike-back to defend themselves, but instead run to disengage themselves from the attacker or seek help. If they met a Muslim, they must walk on their left side, greet them first, and never raise their voice to them.

Even their home must be lower than any Muslim's home, and their Jewish synagogue must not be as high as any Muslim mosque within sight. Yes, even if it forced the local Jewish synagogue to be placed partially underground so it wouldn't be higher than a nearby Muslim mosque.

The law still forbade a Jew to ride a horse or camel that would put them higher than a Muslim, and if they were to ride a donkey or burro they must ride it sitting sideways. If they were to enter a Muslim's house, if they were wearing shoes, they must not forget to remove them and walk bare-footed.

While many of the Muslim imposed rules were almost childish, others covered many things that had serious and lasting consequences. For instance, an earlier Islamic law called the "Orphans' Decree" had been reinstated by the Muslim Imam Yahya in the 1920's. It ordered that any Jewish child under 12 years of age that became an orphan was to be taken-in by a Muslim family and converted to the Muslim religion. It is said that this led to many children under 12 years of age whose parents were dying to become married to an older Jew in order to obviate the "Orphans' Decree."

The months passed and some of the Jewish citizens of Yemen became more and more convinced that the time of the Great Redemption was finally coming. Some became so convinced that the Lord would protect them regardless of what happened that they and their families left their homes, and made their way to the British Protectorate of Aden without any idea what they would do when they got there.

Though the Jewish Yemenites did not have access to newspapers or radios, the news of the founding of Israel and the Arab-Israeli War was trickling in from their rabbi and various other sources. While most Jewish families waited patiently for more news, they became determined that they were going to have a better life, and it was going to be in their promised Jewish homeland. They were not alone. It was estimated, that at the beginning of 1949, there were 900,000 displaced Jewish refugees in Asia and Africa who wanted to be relocated.

The wealthy and powerful Muslim people in Yemen did have radios, and were informed when the Arab-Israeli War had ended. They also knew that Israel had won a decisive military victory. The word had spread and was known by Yemen's then head of government, the Imam Ahmad, and the British in command of the Aden Protectorate. It was not lost on either of them that Israel's proven military prowess in the Middle East, coupled with the power of the financial backing of world-wide organizations, was to be reckoned with realistically, and not to be unnecessarily antagonized. Besides, the United Nations Security Council and Israeli interests had been closely watching and monitoring the displaced refugee's ability to relocate since the end of WW II.

With all this happening, each government began searching for ways to satisfy and appease the powerful interests, solve the refugee problem, and find benefits for themselves at the same time.

Imam Ahmad, of Yemen could accomplish these goals by allowing the Yemenite Jews to leave Yemen, as long as they paid a fee and sold their property and businesses to other Yemenites before they left. That the Yemenite Jews would acquiesce was already demonstrated by the more than 2,000 Yemenites that had already made their way to Aden illegally without permission, while leaving practically everything they owned behind. In the Aden Protectorate, this illegal Yemeni refugee migration was causing a moral and financial problem for the British.

Many of the Yemenite refugees that arrived in Aden had walked barefoot, over a hundred miles to get there. They were defenseless and illegal, and had to pay tribute and fines for passage over many of the local Sultan's territory as they made their way towards Aden. Many arrived illegally in the British Protectorate penniless, thirsty, hungry, sick and worn out, but determined they would somehow find their way to Israel.

Unfortunately, the British had no place to put them, no available medical facilities to treat them, and no money for food to sustain them or personnel to protect them from the local Muslim Arabs. There had been a camp built during WW II to house Italian prisoners of war captured in Eritrea, but it had been destroyed. They needed a camp like that again so the Yemenite refugees could be cared for and protected. Since the war had started, over 80 Jewish people had already been killed by the local Arabs in Aden, and the end of the Israeli-Arab War had not ended their animosity.

Sick or not, the refugees were left without shelter, and sleeping on the desert floor without food or water. They trusted completely in the promise of the Jewish holy book; that they would receive help and find their way to Israel.

The British did what they could with what they had available to care and protect the Yemenite refugees that had arrived, but had to put a stop at the Aden Protectorate's border to prevent any more coming from Yemen to Aden until proper facilities and supplies could be provided. The British also advised Israel that they already had some Jewish Yemenite refugees in dire straights and needed them to be transported to Israel as quickly as possible. For the Yemenite refugees, it was a situation that was a matter of their life or death on the desert sands of the Aden Protectorate

Israel reacted by notifying the International Association of Jewish Refugees of the situation that existed in Aden and asked for their help. The response was quick. Immediate plans began to be laid and the necessary appeals for funding were started. The British and Israel governments both agreed that emergency action needed to be taken at all cost to remove the Yemenite refugees presently in Aden to Israel as soon as possible, and steps be taken to delay future refugees until a camp with protection, shelter, medical attention, sanitation, water and food could be provided.

Israel agreed to pay the expense of building a camp and staffing a medical facility with a doctor and nurses in attendance, along with the cost of sustaining future Yemenite refugees that arrived in Aden until they could be transported to Israel.

The Aden Protectorate agreed to allow the camp to be built, and provide the use of the Khormaksar RAF Station for refugee flights. They would also negotiate with Imam Ahmad of Yemen, and the local Sultans to allow future Yemenite refugees safe passage to the Aden Protectorate. The only request from the British was that the Yemenite refugee program be kept completely secret so it would not upset or bias other British-Arab relations.

A secret agreement had already been reached between the British and Israeli governments on building a camp and facilities to care for the Jewish Yemenite refugees while they were in Aden. Also it was arranged for the American Jewish Joint Distribution Committee (JDC) to provide the financing for the camp and the transportation of the Yemenite Jews by air from the Khormaksar RAF Station in Aden to the Lydda Airport in Israel. The next thing was to arrange for aircraft that could immediately fly the stranded Yemenite refugees in Aden to Israel.

Israel and the American Jewish Joint Distribution Committee (JDC) had already arranged a contract with an American company called Alaska Airlines to fly Jewish refugees from China to Israel. It was March 8, 1949 and there was an Alaska Airlines plane and crew flying from China to Lydda, Israel at the time. The JDC would contact Alaska Airlines to see if there was some way they could possibly use that plane to fly the stranded Yemenite refugees to Israel.

**An Alaska Airlines DC-4 Departing from Seattle Tacoma Airport.
N88756 above, is one of the airplanes we used to fly
the Yemenite Refugees.**
Photo: Alaska Airlines, Courtesy Ed Coates' Civil Aircraft Photograph Collection.

Chapter Two

FROM THE EAST AND THE WEST

> *Fear not: for I am with thee:*
> *I will bring thy seed from the east,*
> *and gather thee from the west*
>
> ***Isaiah 43:5***

My name is Elgen Long and I have an untold story about the Magic Carpet. In 1948 I was hired by Alaska Airlines in New York to navigate their DC-4 aircraft on charter flights across the North Atlantic Ocean to Europe. In January 1949 Alaska Airlines transferred me to Everett, Washington to navigate their DC-4 aircraft on charter flights across the North Pacific Ocean to Asia.

Most of our Alaska Airlines flight-crew were veterans of World War II, and were hired for the various aviation skills that they had developed during the war. In my case, while serving in the U.S. Navy from 1942 to 1946, I had received training as both a flight-navigator and a flight radio-operator.

While I was on my second trip to Asia we were laying over for rest at the Shiba Park Hotel in Tokyo, Japan, when our Captain, Larry Currie, received word that when our crew was rested, we were not to return to Everett, Washington as previously scheduled. Instead, we were to fly to Kai Tak Airport in Hong Kong and check into the Peninsula Hotel in Kowloon. None of our crew, Captain Lawrence "Larry" F. Currie, Co-pilot William "Bill" E. Lester, Navigator Elgen "Al" M. Long, Radio-operator J. Elliot Judd, Flight-mechanic Ralph W. Cheatham, had any idea what we were to do after Hong Kong, nor any inkling that we were destined to participate in one of the great aerial adventures of our time.

Like the young men of aircrews during World War II, we had grown up quickly when faced with the military demands of combat. Almost as habit, we did not question it when our superiors sent us orders, and we tended to treat them as commands, with few questions asked. For just such a contingency, as a navigator, I had collected a complete set of U.S. Air Force navigational charts that covered the world and carried them with me on my trips.

As it turned out, after we had arrived in the British Colony of Hong Kong, we were to stay there for over two weeks before we were finally directed to fly to Shanghai, China's Lunghwa Airport. At Lunghwa, we were to pick-up a plane-load of Jewish refugees that were fleeing from Mao Tze-tung's approaching Communist Army. The trip was to fly the Jewish refugees nearly a third of the way around-the-world to the new State of Israel, that had been formed just a few months before.

Jewish people had lived in China for centuries, but their number had grown exponentially in the 20th century when thousands of Jewish refugees immigrated to China to escape persecution from the governments of the countries in which they had lived and were citizens. As their own countries would not grant them passports or exit visas, many were able to convince Chinese diplomats stationed in their country to give them a visa to travel to and enter China as stateless individuals. Between WW I and the end of WW II, there were thousands of Jewish people who had left their native countries, and traveled to China as stateless refugees.

The Japanese invaded China in 1937, and Shanghai had come under the control and rule of the Japanese Military. The stateless Jewish refugees were closely controlled, but were left as they were until Japan attacked Pearl Harbor on December 7, 1941. When the United States declared war on Japan and the Axis powers, the Japanese military immediately ordered all Americans, British, and stateless Jewish refugees who had not entered China before 1937, into a less than one square mile district that was to become known as the "Shanghai Ghetto."

A few individuals were allowed to remain in their regular residences. One of these was the head of one of the wealthiest families in Asia, Sir Elly Kadoorie. However, his two sons, Lawrence and Horace Kadoorie, were forced to move with their families into the "Shanghai Ghetto." Prior to his death in 1944, Sir Elly Kadoorie, as president of the Palestine Foundation Fund in Shanghai, and his son Horace, who founded the Committee for the Assistance of European Jewish Refugees, were able to provide some aid to the helpless interred refugees.

After WW II ended when Japan surrendered on August 15, 1945, Chiang Kai-shek officially liberated by decree the estimated 8,000 refugees that were restricted to the Ghetto on September 3, 1945, and they were free to leave. Many refugees went to Japan, the United States, and Canada. Some returned to Europe while others migrated to South America and South Africa.

Shortly after WW II ended, backed by Russia, the ranks of the Communist Party in China grew, and soon began a civil war against the government of Generalissimo Chiang Kai-shek.

In Tel Aviv, on Friday, May 14, 1948, the Jewish State of Israel was declared by David Ben-Gurion. When it became possible, many of the remaining Jewish refugees in China wanted to immigrate to the new state of Israel, and flying was the best way they would have to get there. That was why our crew was flying an Alaska Airlines DC-4 on an early morning flight from Hong Kong to Shanghai on Friday, February 18, 1949.

We landed at Shanghai's Lunghwa, Airport located along the bank of the Huang Pu River. (today Lunghwa is closed and has been replaced by two large, and separate, Shanghai International Airports).

The old Lungwha Airport, south of downtown Shanghai by the Huang Pu River.
Photograph © Juha Loukola/flikr.com

After we had cleared customs and immigration, we began preparing the paper work for our departure. We had been informed that most of our Jewish passengers were stateless, with no identity or nationality documentation, and had no passports. We were also advised that as long as we landed at a country friendly to the United States or at an active British Royal Air Force Station, our plane, crew, and passengers would probably be allowed to continue on. But,

11

under no circumstance were we to land, or even flyover, any Muslim country that was at war with Israel.

Using the U.S. Air Force maps I carried, we planned the most practical route to fly our stateless Jewish refugee passengers from Shanghai to Israel. To meet the requirements that would allow safe passage for our stateless passengers, we planned our route from Shanghai, with stops at Bangkok, Calcutta, Bombay, Aden, and finally to Lydda Airport in Israel. Two stewardesses (now known as Flight Attendants) had been provided for the flight, and adding our flight mechanic, Ralph, our two stewardesses, five flight crew members, and 52 passengers, all added up to a total of 60 souls onboard as we departed Shanghai.

Captain Currie had selected to take the maximum amount of fuel we could carry for the flight to Bangkok after considering the weight of the passengers and crew. Ralph had finished the fueling, and we were all ready to board the passengers and go.

As we walked across the airfield ramp toward the airplane, we could see our passengers also coming from the terminal towards the airplane. What surprised us was the way they were dressed. It looked like many of them were wearing more than a single outfit of clothes. Though it wasn't really cold, most had on a heavy shirt, heavy sweaters, a vest, Jacket, and a top coat. Many of the men even had two or three hats stacked on top of their heads. Each passenger had been told they would be allowed only one suitcase, and it could not weigh over 44 pounds.

It was obvious and understandable, that our refugees were trying to take as many personal items with them as they could, but we had an airplane that had to fly without exceeding its maximum allowed weight. The more weight the passengers, the less weight allowed for fuel. The less fuel we had, the less distance we could fly. The flight to Bangkok, Thailand was going to require more fuel than the weight and balance would allow. Captain Currie made the decision we would take-off for Bangkok, and if we were running short of fuel we would make an unscheduled stop in Hong Kong for more fuel.

We took-off from Shanghai about 2:00 p.m. local time, Friday, February 18, 1949, and climbed to our cruising altitude of 8,000 feet. After we leveled-off, and the pilots had set the four engines at cruise power, Captain Currie got out of his pilot's-seat and came back to the navigation station. I laid the map of our route to Bangkok on the chart table, so we could see if there was some way we could make it nonstop. The moon was in its waning phase at about half-full, but it wouldn't come up until around midnight local time.

From over Hong Kong, I had followed the required legal night-route to Bangkok when I had planned the flight, and we were to turn southwest to pass east of Hainan Island. Our route to Bangkok would then take us south of Vietnam and Cambodia, because aircraft could not get clearance to fly over them at night. It was obvious we could not make Bangkok with the fuel we had via the projected route. But, if from Hong Kong we flew to the north of Hainan Island, thru the Hainan Straight into the Gulf of Tonkin, and then headed direct to Bangkok, we would cross Vietnam and Laos at their narrowest points, and fly completely north of Cambodia. If we followed that route, we could make it to Bangkok with the fuel we had on board.

It was February, 1949, and Vietnam and Laos didn't have any radar in operation. Captain Currie made the decision that after Hong Kong we would proceed nonstop, and follow the route north of Hainan and direct to Bangkok. I was to supply Elliot, our radio operator, with time coordinated position reports as if we were flying on our filed route to the south around Vietnam and Cambodia. It was approximately 30 percent shorter via the direct route than the filed route, so I added 30 percent to my groundspeed and listed the times of our filed position reports to Elliot accordingly.

We arrived at Bangkok's Don Muang Airport about 1:00 a.m. local time, Saturday, February 19, 1949. Our next flight was to be to Dum Dum Airport at Calcutta, India, which would take us only a little over 5 hours. It was in the middle of the night and it took longer than usual for the cabin and plane to be serviced. The pilots had been alternating sleeping in the bunks en route, and Elliot and I got a couple of hours sleep while we were on the ground. It was still dark when we left Bangkok, but now it would be late in the morning by the time we arrived in Calcutta. I was hoping the facilities at Dum Dum would be suitable for me to get a chance to shave and wash-up, while we were there.

The flight went as planned, and en route to Calcutta I was able to complete the flight plan for the next leg of our flight from Calcutta to Bombay.

After landing at Dum Dum Airport in Calcutta, I took my shaving kit into the terminal to brush my teeth and shave. I found a wash basin that was available, and turned on the water spigot to wet my toothbrush. Instead of water coming from the end of the spigot, a cockroach crawled out. I put my toothbrush and razor back in my kit bag, and returned to the plane. Ralph Cheatham was there refueling, and I asked him to have somebody wake me an hour before we reached Bombay. The pilots could navigate by radio from Calcutta to Bombay, and it was my turn in the bunk. I was asleep in minutes, and only vaguely remember hearing the engines roar when we took-off from Calcutta.

Before I knew it, I was awakened by Ralph, and told we were an hour out of Bombay. I got up and went to the cockpit to layout our flight from Bombay to Aden, and fill out the flight plan. We arrived in Bombay, and all I needed was the winds aloft forecast, so I could calculate our time en route. We had developed a routine that was working well, and our progress was as good as we could reasonably have expected.

Flying from Bombay to the Khormaksar RAF Station in the British Aden Protectorate was going to take us about ten hours, and the nearest suitable alternate airport was about two hours further away. Every other alternate was in an Arab country's territory, where we couldn't land with the stateless Jewish passengers onboard. The weather forecast for Aden and our alternate, Asmara, Eritrea was very good, so Captain Currie decided to take-off with our maximum allowable load of fuel, even though we would be a little short of the required holding reserve, if we had to divert from Aden to our alternate. After take-off from Bombay, we set our course just to the south of the Kuria Muria Islands, off the coast of Oman. From there, we stayed well-off the coast of the Arabian Peninsula, until we came to the Khormaksar RAF Station at Aden.

We arrived at Khormaksar before noon, but it was mid-afternoon by the time we finished refueling and were ready to go. We were at the maximum weight for take-off and would have to take-off in the heat of the day. It would also be dark by the time we arrived at Lydda. Captain Currie decided we should take 12 hours to get mandatory rest in Aden, and take-off in the cool of the morning, about daylight the next day.

During the flight from Bombay, I had gotten out the charts covering our next flight, and searched for a route that would not take us over any Arab countries, when we flew from Aden to Lydda, Israel. The Red Sea was lined on both sides by Muslim nations that were, except for Sudan, in a state of war with Israel. The narrow entrance from the Gulf of Aden into the southern end of the Red Sea was further narrowed by Perim Island, while Egypt's Sinai Peninsula completely blocked its' northern end.

From Sunday school, I remembered Moses was able to lead the Israelites across the northern end of Red Sea to Sinai and the Negev desert without the Egyptian army of the Pharaoh's being able to attack them. Our problem was much the same, except instead of just across its northern end, to keep from being attacked by the Israeli enemy's armies, we had to fly the full length of the Red Sea, from one end to the other, without being detected.

From Khormaksar we could fly off the coast of Yemen in the Gulf of Aden, and enter the Red Sea at Perim Island that was under British control. From there, as we flew north, if we stayed equal distance from the Saudi Arabian coast to our east, and the Egyptian coast to our west, we stood a good chance of remaining undetected.

The northern end of the Red Sea was blocked by the Sinai Peninsula, and the waters of the Red Sea split into two gulfs. To the northwest, was the Gulf of the Suez that led to the Suez Canal, and to the northeast, the Gulf of Aqaba that led to a narrow Israeli held strip of land on the northwestern shore, at the its northeastern end.

By flying up the center of the Gulf of Aqaba, we could reach Israeli territory where the city of Eilat is now located. From there, we could fly over Israeli controlled territory, up the Negev Desert to Beersheba, and on to Lydda Airport, where we were to deliver our passengers.

It was going to take us about nine hours to fly to Lydda, and the operations officer at Khormaksar, advised us we would probably not be able to get aviation fuel at Lydda and would need enough extra fuel to fly from Lydda to the RAF Base located at Nicosia, on the Island of Cyprus. This meant we would need about 2700 gallons of fuel onboard for departure, and with that heavy a load, wouldn't be able to take-off until the next morning, when the temperature would be cooler.

We were flying in the Tropic of Cancer, where the weather was mild and quite predictable in the late winter and early spring. A little before sunrise the temperature is coolest at about 65 degrees Fahrenheit and it steadily gets warmer as the day progresses to a high of about 88 degrees Fahrenheit around 5:00 p.m. As the temperature increases, the density of the air decreases. This causes the lift from the wings and power from the aircraft's engines to decrease and a longer runway is required for take-off.

Captain Currie had already decided we would wait until morning, and arranged for a crew bus to take us to the Crescent Hotel in Aden. We were actually going to get 12 hours rest in a hotel, for the first time since leaving Hong Kong three days ago. We were to be awakened at 3:00 a.m.

It was still dark, when we gathered for tea and finger sandwiches in the hotel lobby, shortly before 4:00 a.m. Thirty minutes later, we were all back on the crew bus heading for Khormaksar and an early morning take-off for Israel.

As we travelled towards the RAF Station, morning twilight was starting to illuminate our surroundings. I was amazed to see natives crawling out of caves in the extinct volcano Al-Akhbar's cliffs, along the roadside, where they obviously lived. This was the second revelation of the native population I had noticed since arriving in Aden. Earlier, I had noticed many of the men had red stained teeth,

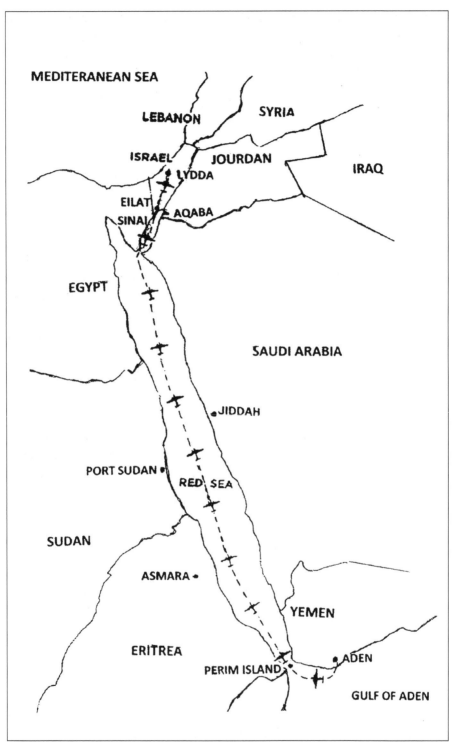

Map of our flights from Aden to Lydda with Yemenite Refugees.
Drawn by Elgen M. Long

mouths, and lips. I learned the chewing of betel nuts was very common, and it was the juice from the betel nut leaves that caused the red staining.

When we arrived at Khormaksar, Bill Lester, Ralph Cheatham, and the stewardesses went to the plane to start their preflight inspections, while Captain Currie, Judd, and I went to the operations office to get the latest weather, notices to airmen, and file our flight plan.

A cablegram from our company had been sent to Khormaksar, and the Operations Officer had Captain Currie sign a receipt for it. The message was from the Alaska Airlines office in New York. Captain Currie read the message, and said we were to proceed to Schiphol Airport at Amsterdam, Netherlands, after delivering our passengers to Lydda, Israel.

The operations officer had our winds and weather forecast ready, and everything looked good. When we finished studying the weather, the operations officer, reiterated the earlier warning we had received about avoiding Arab countries at war with Israel when carrying Jewish passengers. He even went so far as to suggest, that in case of an emergency requiring an immediate landing while flying over the Red Sea, we might consider ditching alongside a European ship, rather than heading to land on any Arab country's shore.

We were about ready to have the passengers boarded, when Ralph came into the office, and informed Captain Currie that he had found an engine-oil leak that would require a couple of hours to fix. It was already getting daylight outside, and the temperature would rise as the morning went on. The operations officer ordered an engine work-stand be taken out to the plane for the mechanic to work on. There was nothing we could do but wait while Ralph fixed the oil leak.

It was nearly 11:00 a.m., when Ralph said he had fixed the leak and wanted the pilots to run the engine, so he could check that everything was okay. Captain Currie and Bill went out to the plane to conduct the engine run-up for Ralph. A short time later, we could hear the engine start and run for a few minutes. Captain Currie came back from the plane, and asked that the passenger be brought out and boarded onto the plane for departure. He was anxious to get off before the temperature got any higher.

The operations officer had changed since we had first been briefed, and he accepted the flight plan we filed as if we were going to Nicosia, Cypress. He also informed us that there was a radio-beacon on Perim Island and at Jeddah in Saudi Arabia that aircraft could use for radio direction-finding and gave us the frequencies and identification codes for both beacons. The officer then added that there was no peace agreement that had officially been signed by Israel with Egypt, Jordan, Lebanon, Saudi Arabia, or Syria. Israel was still at war with all those countries. If we were to land in any of those countries, our passengers would be in immediate danger, and our American crew and plane were likely to be at least interred. He also told us we might not want to log our stops into Israel and to avoid getting any Israeli stamp in our passports or on any other of our paperwork. Anything Israeli, in our passports or logs, would complicate the situation if we were forced to land in an Arab country.

With Israel still on a war-footing everything was done in secrecy. Our flight would not be announced, nor would there be anything reported about it on the radio, in the newspapers, or anywhere else. No other flights, if any, would know about us, and we would know nothing about them. During the flight from Aden to Israel, with the Jewish refugees onboard, we were pretty much on our own.

We knew that Israel had shot down five British RAF aircraft the month before on January 7, 1949, in Israeli controlled airspace. Though I did not know it at the time, two of the Israeli Defense Force pilots involved were future Flying Tiger Line pilots Wayne Peake, and Chalmers H. "Slick" Goodlin, a test pilot with Bell Aircraft and later a pilot with Near East Air Transport. I was to know both of them later. It was sobering to realize it was possible we could meet a similar fate to the British Aircraft if we were detected or strayed over Arab territory.

International flight crews have sustained habits they have developed over time in the way they handle confusing or contradictory information. In general, because they are often flying into a place they have never been before, they quite diligently stick to the written word in their charts and books, and changes are not accepted until they are revised and distributed to them in written form in those charts and books. We must remember that as our flight to Israel was being made on Monday, February 21, 1949, Israel was in the middle of a war, and had been in existence for less than a year. Lots of things had changed, but not much of it had gotten into print and distributed throughout the world to international flight crews.

So it was with Lydda Airport in Israel. Shortly after Israel was declared a state, the Israelis changed the name of the town of Lydda, back to its biblical name of "Lod." At the same time, they also changed the name of "Lydda Airport" to "Lod Airport." However, in February, 1949, nothing much had been changed on the charts and books the international flight crews used, and during the time we were flying the flights into Israel everyone still called it "Lydda Airport." I will use the name "Lydda Airport" while writing about these flights.

At the time this is being written in 2015, "Lydda Airport" is now named "Ben-Gurion Airport," and it is one of the largest and busiest airports in the

Middle East. The change was made to honor Israel's first Prime Minister, David Ben-Gurion, after his death in December of 1973. If you have flown into Tel Aviv, Israel's Ben-Gurion Airport since 1973, you flew into the same airport we called Lydda in 1949. All present day aviation charts and books have it identified in print as Ben-Gurion Airport.

We all went out to the plane, where we found Ralph at the navigators table writing up the repair work he had done on the engine in the ship's logbook. The passengers were being boarded by the stewardesses (now known as flight-attendants), and the pilots had started their preflight check list. The cabin finally reported our Shanghai passengers were ready for departure, and the pilots started our engines.

It was near noon local time when we were finally able to take-off from Khormaksar. We turned out over the Gulf of Aden and headed westward towards Perim Island and the southern mouth of the Red Sea. Our flight plan predicted we would have nearly a nine-hour flight from Aden to Lydda Airport in Israel, and because of the mechanical delay we would not be arriving until about an hour after sunset.

The beacon on Perim Island worked well for our radio direction-finder to home on, and we entered the southern end of the Red Sea right on flight plan. We picked up a heading that would keep us flying up the middle of the Red Sea until we got to its northern end at the Egyptian Sinai Peninsula. I took drift sights with our B-4 drift-meter and adjusted our headings to the left or right as required to maintain our course up the middle of the Red Sea.

As we went by Jidda on the Saudi Arabian coast, we tuned in the beacon at Jidda and I made what navigators call a running fix by timing how long it took for the beacon to go from 45 degrees off to our right until it was directly abeam 90 degrees off on our right side. It had taken 15 minutes to go from 45 to 90 degrees, and by triangulation with a groundspeed of about 200 mph in 15 minutes we had traveled about 50 miles. So at the time the beacon was 90 degrees off to our right we were 50 miles offshore from the radio beacon at Jidda.

Unfortunately, I didn't have an accurate chronometer to supply me with the exact time for taking celestial observation. WWV time-ticks from the United States (WWV radio marked the precise time with dots and dashes on several frequencies) could not always be received. The running radio-fix was not as accurate as a celestial observation, but a lot better than nothing.

Several hours later, when we spotted the coast of the Sinai Peninsula ahead, we turned to the right and stayed well offshore. Though we had not planned it, as we approached the mouth of the Gulf of Aqaba the sun was behind us and low on the horizon. This would make it difficult for anyone on the Egyptian Islands in the mouth of the gulf to see us from the ground as we approached. From here on Elliot was not to contact any of the Egyptian or Arab radio stations.

We entered the gulf offshore and flew at 8,500 feet through the Strait of Tiran staying equal distance from the Sinai coast and the Island of Jazirat Tiran. The Gulf of Aqaba averaged only about 15 miles in width, so we could see the shoreline on both sides as we flew up the middle of the gulf towards its' northeastern end.

About halfway up the gulf, Elliot reported he had not been able to make contact with the Israeli radio station at Lydda. Captain Currie told him he would try to make contact on VHF frequencies with voice from the cockpit when he got nearer to Beersheba.

The sun was getting lower and lower in the sky behind us as we made our way up the gulf towards Aqaba in Jordan. The city of Aqaba was only about 10 miles to the southeast across the gulf from where we would enter Israeli territory on the opposite northwestern shore. As we neared the end of the gulf we could see a small British Naval Vessel that appeared to be docked there. It must have had radar on board, and we probably had already been detected by it. We could only trust the British didn't want to get even for the RAF Spitfire fighters and Mosquito bomber that Israel had shot down the month before.

When we were almost at the northeastern end of the Gulf, and the port of Aqaba in Jourdan was off to our right, we turned left and headed almost due north across the Sinai Desert towards Beersheba. The sun had disappeared below the horizon, and it was going to be moonless and completely dark in less than 30 minutes. I estimated it would take us 37 minutes to reach Beersheba, and 33 minutes more to reach the Lydda airport. To arrive over Lydda at 1,000 feet above the airport we should start our descent of 350 feet a minute from 8,500 feet, 12 minutes after leaving Beersheba.

The evening twilight dimmed right on schedule, and by the time we passed over Beersheba it was completely dark outside. The pilots had no luck on the VHF radio, and Elliot had not been able to raise Lydda or any Israeli station on his radio. We had no late weather report for Lydda, however so far the visibility outside was good and the pilot's eyes had adjusted to the dark. Captain Currie started our descent 12 minutes after passing over Beersheba while flying the heading that would take us directly to the Lydda Airport.

The airport was about 12 miles southeast of the city of Tel Aviv and the pilots in the darkened cockpit should be able to see the lights of the city off to their left as we approached it. The pilots had called Lydda on the tower frequency of 126.18 and asked them to turn on the airport lights, but received no answer. About 10 minutes before we were due to arrive they could see Tel Aviv ahead and off to the left, but no airport lights for Lydda were in sight. We had enough gas to fly to Nicosia, and I had already worked out the compass heading from Lydda to Nicosia; just in case.

We reached the estimated time of arrival for Lydda, but the pilots could not see any signs of the airport. Captain Currie began a circle to the left looking for the airport lights when he spotted the outline of a runway in the dark. There were no runway lights lit on it, but he could see well enough to tell it was a paved runway at an airport. He reduced power and called for gear down, and adjusted his turn to enter a flight pattern that would bring him back to the runway in line for an approach so he could land on the unlit runway. As the plane slowed he lowered the flaps to 15 degrees. When he was lined up with the runway on final approach he turned on our planes landing lights, and lowered the flaps to 35 degrees for landing. Captain Currie then adjusted his descent and speed so we would touchdown near the approach end of the runway. Using just the planes landing lights he made a good landing and came to a moderately rapid but smooth stop. We had landed at Lydda about 8:00 p.m. local time, Monday, February 21, 1949.

The pilots were looking about for a building that looked like it might be an airport terminal, when they noticed the lights of a vehicle coming across the airport towards them. It drove up in front of us to act as a follow-me vehicle, and led us to the terminal ramp where we were signaled to park. After we had come to a stop we could see what we had been following wasn't a follow-me truck, it was an armored car.

When the engines were shut-down, we could hear cheers from the passenger cabin as our passengers celebrated their arrival in Israel. It had been quite a trip from Shanghai for them, as well as for us.

No stairs were brought to the plane, and we didn't open any doors in case they wanted to spray the interior of the plane with DDT to kill any odd bugs that might have hitched a ride with us along the way. Someone on the ramp shined a flashlight at the captain's side window. Captain Currie slid his side window open, and stuck his head out. The man on the ramp asked if we wanted a ladder put up to the plane so we could get out. Currie answered we had passengers from Shanghai on board and they needed a stair-ramp to get off. The ramp man said he didn't have access to stairs, but he would get us a ladder and bring it to the cabin door.

We opened the cabin door, and soon a ladder was put in place to it. A man in a uniform came up the ladder into the cabin and came forward to the cockpit. Captain Currie told him we had flown our passengers from Shanghai, China, and had just flown nonstop from Khormaksar RAF Station in Aden. He had a walkie-talkie and radioed something in a foreign language. There was a short answer, and he told us that they would offload the passengers and their baggage onto the ramp and officials would be arriving soon to process them. He also thanked us for bringing the refugees safely to Israel from the Far East, and remarked. "It is a good thing you have done!"

Ralph asked if we could get an electrical power-cart to plug into the plane to provide us with electricity. The Israeli army officer after talking into the walkie-talkie for a moment said a power-cart was on its way. Ralph left to go down the ladder to put in the gear-pins (three pins that when inserted into the three landing gear mechanisms kept them from retracting), check the wheel-chocks were in place (wedged wooden blocks put in front and back of the tires to keep them from rolling), and make sure the power-cart was plugged in properly when it came.

We asked the Israeli officer if transportation would be available for the passengers. He said thousands of refugees have been arriving monthly, and the refugee organization is prepared to arrange transportation to take them to a refugee center where they would be processed and taken care of. As soon as the passengers and their luggage were off-loaded from the plane our responsibility for them would end.

While we were waiting an Israeli radioman from the airport came to the plane and explained that they had heard all of Elliot's radio-calls, but the airport was under an alert for a possible attack, and restrictions required by the war prevented him from answering or transmitting the weather report on the radio. In the future, when we were en route to Lydda if we called them, they would answer with a single letter of the alphabet. The single letter in Morse Code would signal that they were not under attack and the weather was suitable for landing. It could be any letter except "X." If the letter sent was "X," it signaled that you should not approach or land at Lydda, but proceed to an alternate airport.

Captain Currie thanked the radioman, and told the Army Officer we would leave for Amsterdam as soon as we refueled and filed our flight plan. The Army Officer nodded, and talked again for a few moments on the walkie-talkie. An answer came back in a few minutes informing us that because of the war they had no 100 octane aviation gas available to refuel us.

Armored cars at Lydda Airport in Lydda, Israel.

Captain Currie looked at me, and asked how long it would take us to fly to Nicosia? I answered that it would take about an hour-and-a-half. We still had nearly a hundred-and-fifty gallons in each of the four main tanks, and with the airplane empty that would last us at least three hours. Captain Currie said we would check the latest weather, and if it was good we would go with the fuel onboard. I handed him the flight plan I made to Nicosia, and asked them to wake me when necessary. Elliot was already in the top bunk, but the bottom bunk was empty. I took off my shoes and climbed into it, and was sound asleep within minutes. Evidently the pilots didn't feel it was necessary to wake me, as I slept all the way to Nicosia.

When we started refueling at Nicosia, I calculated the flight plan to Amsterdam. Our flight was going to take us a little over ten hours. We would burn 2040 gallons en route, plus carry 480 gallons extra for taxi and take-off and have Brussels, Belgium as an alternate, and reserve fuel for holding. The total minimum fuel required was 2520 gallons, and Captain Currie elected to fuel the plane with 2600 gallons.

We took off from Nicosia a little after midnight local time on Monday, February 21, 1949, via Greece, Italy, Austria, and Germany to Amsterdam. We landed at Amsterdam's Schiphol Airport about 10:00 a.m. local time Tuesday, February 22, 1949.

Schiphol was a major terminal for both trans-Atlantic and European flights, and served almost all the major airlines. After landing we were cleared to taxi to the KLM maintenance area where we parked next to one of their large maintenance hangers, and shut down our engines. A power-cart was immediately available, and a stand with stairs was pushed up to the cabin door. After we had written up any of the aircraft's systems that needed servicing or repair, and completed the log book, Captain Currie signed it and handed it to Ralph.

Ralph would stay with the plane to supervise the maintenance and come to the hotel later. We packed up our flight gear, grabbed our suitcases, and headed for an Amsterdam hotel. Captain Currie had received a cablegram advising us that we were to return to Israel with a partial load of Jewish refugees. On the way we were to stop in Rome to pick-up another partial load comprising of a ship's crew going to Manila, in the Philippines. Then from Manila we were to return to Hong Kong. He also advised us we would probably be leaving from Amsterdam about 10:00 p.m. local time, and should meet at the hotel for dinner at 7:00 p.m.

The plane was to be refueled to 2600 gallons, after Rome we would have to stop again at Nicosia for fuel before going on to Lydda. While Ralph stayed with the plane to oversee the work that the KLM mechanics did on our plane, the rest of the crew took 12 hours legal rest in a nearby Amsterdam Hotel. This gave us a chance to bathe, get some laundry done, sleep in a real bed, and enjoy a good hot meal. I pulled the covers up close around my neck as northern Europe was much cooler in February than it had been at our previous stops in the more southern latitudes.

The last thing I remembered before going sound asleep were the cheers of joy that the refugees from Shanghai expressed when we landed in Israel, and the words of the Israeli Officer when he thanked us for bringing the refugees home. "It is a good thing you have done!"

I am sure as we slept soundly in our hotel none of us even dreamed that the next time we were to come to Amsterdam we would be participating in flights that were to lead to a historic change in the history and lives of hundreds of thousands of refugees.

Chapter Three

FROM THE NORTH AND THE SOUTH

> *I will say to the north, Give up;*
> *and to the south, Keep not back:*
> *bring my sons from far, and my daughters*
> *from the ends of the earth.*
>
> **Isaiah 43:6**

Twelve hours after we had arrived in Amsterdam, we were back at Schiphol Airport getting ready for our return flight south to Israel and Aden, then eastward to the Philippines, and China. Unfortunately, we were delayed a couple of hours because one of the mechanical repairs KLM had made to the airplane did not checkout during our preflight check, and had to be redone by their mechanics.

We departed Amsterdam before midnight on Tuesday, February 22, 1949 for Rome with a partial-load of Jewish refugees bound for Lydda, Israel. In Rome we picked up an Italian ship's crew of seamen that were on their way to join their ship in Manila. We did not need to refuel in Rome, and after little more than an hour on the ground at Rome's Ciampino Airport we took-off for Nicosia. As there was no fuel available for us in Lydda, we were going to have to leave from Nicosia with enough fuel for both the flight to Lydda, and the flight from Lydda on to Aden. The weight and balance for the flight from Nicosia gave us a problem in reverse of the usual one of not to exceed the maximum weight for take-off weight. This time the problem was not to exceed the maximum landing-weight at Lydda. Thanks to the DC-4's broad range of capabilities, it finally worked out that we would not exceed any of the aircrafts' weight restrictions for landing.

We landed in Nicosia shortly after noon local time, and were airborne for Lydda with 2750 gallons of fuel onboard before 3:00 p.m. This time it was daylight when we arrived at Lydda, and the airport operation was efficient and normal. Again, the refugees onboard were very excited and effusive in their thanks for our having brought them to their new home in Israel.

We were only on the ground about an hour in Lydda, and it was still daylight when we took-off for Aden. We left Lydda with only the Italian ship's crew onboard as passengers, and headed direct to Beersheba to retrace the reverse of the routing we had made when we had flown into Lydda from Aden. The pilots leveled-off at 9,500 feet and the flight to Aden proceeded as planned.

After flying 65 hours from Amsterdam to Rome, Nicosia, Lydda, Aden, Bombay, Calcutta, Singapore, Manila, we arrived back in Hong Kong on Saturday, February 26, 1949. We had flown 126 hours during the eight days since we had left Hong Kong, and had averaged nearly 16 hours of flying per day. That many hours of flight-operations without legal rest periods would not be acceptable today, but in 1948 and early 1949 it was sometimes necessary under the exigent conditions that we faced.

At Hong Kong we checked in again to the Peninsula Hotel in Kowloon, and were scheduled to fly to Shanghai on March 1st.

While we were in Hong Kong, I shopped for a chronometer so I could have the exact time available to make accurate celestial observations on our flights, regardless of the time of day or where we were. I went looking for a pocket watch type Chronometer like we used in the Navy, but luckily found a much handier waterproof Rolex Oyster Perpetual wristwatch that was also a certified chronometer.

The ROLEX Certified Chronometer I bought in Hong Kong.
Elgen M. Long Collection.

As scheduled, on Tuesday, March 1, 1949 we flew from Hong Kong to Shanghai in a little over four hours. At Lunghwa Airport in Shanghai, Alaska Airline's Captain John Thompson and his crew were waiting for our plane to arrive. They were to fly a flight of Jewish refugees to Israel on the plane we flew in for them from Hong Kong. We were to wait in Shanghai approximately seven days for Captain Thompson to return, and then we would make another flight with the plane loaded with Jewish refugees homeward bound to Israel.

Before we left for the hotel in Shanghai, Captain Currie talked at length with Captain Thompson about what we had learned on our trip as did Ralph with Thompson's mechanic about the condition of the aircraft. Afterward we cleared customs and immigration and loaded our bags onto our crew bus that would take us from the Lunghwa airport to our Shanghai hotel.

On the way I checked the amount of money I had left in my wallet. After buying my Rolex chronometer, and having already been away from home for nearly two months, I was nearly out of money. Captain Currie carried company cash to provide advances to crew members for per diem expenses when necessary, and he advanced me enough money to hopefully cover my personal expenses for the remainder of our trip.

The Cathay Mansion was our hotel, and it was conveniently located where we could walk the Bund along the Yangtze River watching the acrobats, jugglers, beggars, and street merchants do their thing. Shops, restaurants, and clubs were all nearby, and I had a chance to visit the favorite club of some of the Flying Tiger pilots of World War II fame; some of whom were still flying in China for CNAC and General Claire Chennault's CAT airlines in March of 1949.

One evening, Elliot and I went to see a theatre production in the French Concession Area of Shanghai. The play was "Born Yesterday," it was in English, very good and very funny. The actor who played "Harry Brock," the junkyard millionaire, and the actress who was his girlfriend "Billie Dawn" were sensational. It was surprising to find a top New York City Broadway hit play being so well performed in Shanghai, China.

On the more serious side of life, inflation of China's Gold Yuan currency was rampant. The Chinese Republic had issued a new currency that was advertised to be as good as gold, and it was mandatory for all Chinese citizens to exchange any gold or foreign currency they possessed for the government's new paper Gold Yuan currency. A citizen who did not comply, and was found with gold or foreign currency could be very severely punished.

While the Gold Yuan started at one to one equal with the U.S. dollar, the story goes that as the Communist troops advanced ever closer, it soon took a wheelbarrow to carry enough Gold Yuan to buy lunch.

On the really serious side of Shanghai's problems, during the night I would leave my hotel room window open to let in a cool breeze. One night the wind must have changed direction, because when I woke I could hear the karrummmp! Karrummmp! that I recognized from my World War II days as the sound of cannon and mortar fire from a battle in progress in the distance. It seemed most likely Shanghai's days under the Chinese Republic were numbered.

The week had passed quickly, and we found ourselves on Tuesday, March 8, 1949 back at Lunghwa Airport filing our flight plan for Bangkok. We were on our way again with a load of stateless Jewish refugees flying them westward towards their new home in Israel.

With my new chronometer providing the correct time, I could navigate celestially across any ocean. On this trip we calculated that we could save some flight time and avoid one stop by proceeding from Bangkok direct to the British RAF Station of Ratmalana near Colombo, Ceylon, now called Sri Lanka. Then from Colombo we could fly direct to Aden. It was a good plan and less than eight hours after leaving Bangkok we were landing in Colombo.

The flight from Colombo to Aden was going to take nearly 13 hours and it would require all the fuel we could carry with our load of refugees. Captain Currie calculated the minimum required fuel load was 3000 gallons, and had the plane refueled accordingly. The servicing was completed and we were ready for takeoff by 11:00 a.m. local time.

We taxied out to the active runway and the windsock was limp, indicating that there was very little wind blowing down the runway. Beyond the end of the runway we could see a line of palm trees along the beach near the shoreline of the Laccadive Sea. The RAF tower cleared us for take-off, and the pilots applied take-off power to the engines. Our plane slowly gained speed as we went down the runway. The acceleration seemed to be normal, but as we were nearing the end of the runway we were still not airborne. The pilot brought the nose up and we broke ground just before we reached the runway's end. The nose was higher than normal, and it looked like the palm trees were going to pass below us as the landing-gear was selected for retraction.

As soon as we were over the water the pilots slowly lowered the nose, and gained more airspeed before climbing higher and retracting the flaps. Once we were safely several hundred feet in the air, and the airspeed had increased to normal climb speed, they reduced the engine settings to climb-power while continuing our climb to 8,000 feet. Reaching 8,000 feet we leveled-off (maintained the current-altitude) and increased to our normal cruise indicated airspeed of 170 mph. The pilots then set cruise power, and shifted the engine carburetor mixture controls to auto-lean.

The flight across the Laccadive and Arabian Seas was routine. Even during daylight when the sun, Venus or the moon are available, with my new Rolex chronometer I always had the correct time for taking celestial observations. That definitely was going to make my navigation more dependable and accurate.

We landed at Khormaksar RAF Station in Aden about 11:00 p.m. local time. Ralph had deplaned to insert the gear pins, and check the power cart. Our passengers were deboarded so the cabin facilities could be serviced and cleaned, and to give the passengers a chance to stretch their legs.

As soon as he could, Ralph came back into the plane and asked Captain Currie to come out and look at the plane's landing gear. Co-pilot Bill and I followed them down onto the ramp. As we walked forward towards the main landing gear we could see there were parts of palm fronds stuck and wrapped around both of the main landing-gear struts and gear doors. It was obvious we had dragged the landing gear through the top of the palm trees during the take-off from Ratmalana. Ralph and Captain Currie agreed the fronds would all have to be removed and the gear struts, doors, tires, hydraulics, and electrical parts inspected before we could continue. Ralph estimated with some help from the RAF he could get the inspection completed in four or five hours, and if nothing was found damaged, we would be able to take-off again by 6:00 or 7:00 a.m.

We went to the operations office to prepare our flight plan and see if we could get some help for Ralph with the gear inspection. The RAF Operations Officer said he would send out a couple of duty mechanics to help Ralph, and had Captain Currie sign for a cablegram from Alaska Airlines.

The message indicated we were to deliver our passengers to Lydda, refuel, take 12 hours rest, and return to Aden for further instructions.

We hoped to take-off early enough to reach Lydda before dark. It was 6:00 a.m. in the morning before Ralph reported the palm fronds had been removed and the inspection had found no damage to the landing gear. The plane had already been refueled to the required fuel load of 2600 gallons.

Captain Currie, Radio officer Elliot, and I got the latest updates of the weather and filed our flight plan, while Bill went out to the plane to start the pre-flight and check with Ralph on the work he had done.

The winds aloft forecast showed some headwinds going to Lydda, and it was going to take us about ten hours en route. Before we filed our flight plan, the RAF Officer added to our briefing the information that since our last flight from Aden to Israel, Egypt had signed a separate Armistice agreement with Israel on February 24th, but no Armistice agreement had yet been signed with Saudi Arabia, Jordan, Lebanon, or Syria.

We decided not to file an instrument flight plan with air traffic control, and just file a visual flight plan from Aden to Lydda. That way no radio contacts or position reports would be required. We would follow the same flight plan as before up the Red Sea to the Sinai Peninsula, and up the Gulf of Aqaba to the Israeli controlled territory at its' north-eastern end. Elliot would not have to make any position reports, and could contact the Israeli station at Lydda whenever Captain Currie wanted him to check the "one-letter" Lydda condition report.

The passengers were onboard, and we were ready to go. A little before 8:00 a.m. local time we finally became airborne from Khormaksar. We turned right over the Gulf of Aden and headed offshore towards Perim Island and the mouth of the Red Sea. Our flight plan predicted we would have a ten-hour flight from Aden to Lydda airport in Israel, and even so, it looked like this time we would be arriving well before sunset.

Elliot was able to get a radio time check from WWV, and over a period of two days my Rolex was only two-seconds off. That was as good, or better, than the navy chronometers I had during WW II. Confident now that I had the right time, I took shots of the sun as it passed our meridian to the south of us. With my A-10 octant I kept measuring the elevation of the sun as it rose-higher in the sky, and caught the exact time when it started to descend. The time when the sun is the highest in sky is called local apparent noon. By looking in my almanac on the date and exact time the sun was highest, it will list the longitude of the sun at that moment, which would also be our planes longitude at that moment. The sextant, or octant, at the same time is measuring the exact altitude the sun is above the horizon, and by comparing that with my almanac of the sun's declination (the same as the earth's latitude that the sun is over) I could compute the latitude of our airplane. Behold! We have an accurate fix of the latitude and longitude of where our plane was located at that moment using just the sun.

This would be a very important asset if we were flying above clouds and could not see if we were over land. Especially as we approach the Sinai Peninsula and must turn to go up the rather narrow Gulf of Aqaba. As navigator, I felt much relieved by having constant access to the exact time.

About 4:00 p.m. local time, we came near to the northern end of the Gulf of Aqaba, and the Port of Aqaba was off to our right, we turned left and headed north to Beersheba. Captain Currie asked Elliot to call Lydda and see what letter of the alphabet they answered with.

Elliot turned on the Collins ART-13 transmitter and warmed it up. He just had to call Lydda once, and they answered simply with the single Morse-code letter "G." It was not "X" and Elliot reported to Captain Currie that indicated it was alright for us to proceed on into Lydda Airport.

As the single letter report had indicated, the weather was good and the airport operations were normal when we landed a little after 5:00 p.m. local time, Thursday, March 10, 1949 at the Lydda Airport.

The Jewish refugees from Shanghai, who after years of exile as stateless refugees had finally made it home to Israel. The cheers from the cabin expressed their relief and happiness.

What we did not know then, and seemed no one was aware of until now, our flight of Jewish refugees from Shanghai, China by happenstance, were at, or very near, Umm Rashrash (now Eilat) when "The Ink Flag" was raised at 16:00 hours, (4:00 p.m.) March 10, 1949. The raising of "The Ink Flag" has become known as the symbolic signal of the end of the 1948-1949 Arab-Israeli War. How appropriate it was that the refugees from Shanghai had arrived home in Israeli territory at the time and place of that very event.

At least they had the distinction of being the first refugees to arrive in Israel after the Arab-Israeli War ended. Also, they most likely shared with us having arrived at Lydda on the first international passenger flight to arrive after the raising of the Israeli "Ink Flag" at Umm Rashrash, later renamed Eilat.

A new cablegram from Alaska Airlines in New York instructed us to take legal rest in Tel Aviv. The stewardesses were to stay in Tel Aviv, but after legal rest our flight-crew was to return to Aden and wait for further instructions.

A crew-bus was arranged to take us to Tel Aviv, and when we told the airport authority we would be leaving in 12 hours, we were surprised when they asked how much fuel we would need. Captain Currie questioned if they meant that they now had fuel available? Their answer was yes. They figured our flight must be important because they had been instructed to furnish us with whatever fuel we needed.

Before we left for the hotel in Tel Aviv, Captain Currie told Ralph to fuel the plane to 2600 gallons.

At the hotel over dinner, we couldn't help but ponder why we were told to return to Aden, and why fuel was suddenly made available to us for the flight. Maybe the gas man at Lydda was right. Something important might be in the works.

Ralph had also reached the hotel, and we were all asleep before 8:00 p.m. with wakeup time set for 3:00 a.m. Captain Currie wanted us to take-off for Aden by sunrise.

I'm afraid that the rest you get when sleeping on the plane en route does not compare to sleeping in a real-bed in a quiet room. The knock of the clerk on the door at 3:00 a.m. came much too soon. A quick bath, shave, and fresh clothes made waking up a little better, but just a little. Our usual routine was a quick snack substituted for the usual full breakfast, back to your room, pack your suitcase, down to the lobby, pay your hotel bill, and climb into the crew bus for the trip to Lydda airport.

The winds aloft had lightened up a little since yesterday, and our flight plan estimated it would take us about eight hours to fly back to Aden. We filed a Visual Flight Rules flight plan to Aden via the reverse of the routing that we had come to Lydda on. There was no further cablegram or word on what we were to do when we got to Aden, and it looked like we would just have to wait till we got there to find out what it was. Without passengers to board we were ready to go quicker than usual and were actually able to depart Lydda in the early morning light before 6:00 a.m. Friday, March 11, 1949.

As usual this time of year the weather was good for flying, and we were getting used to the intricate demands of our routing. Without position reports to make, Elliot felt like a fifth wheel. As long as the weather remained good, navigation was mostly taking drift-sights to stay on course, and checking our progress as we arrived at the entrances to the Red Sea and the Gulf of Aqaba. Except for the night time blackout at Lydda the first time we had arrived there, the Arab-Israeli War had so far only provided us with a threatening environment.

We realized the significance of the cease-fire agreement declared by the Arab and Israeli forces, and were aware that a formal armistice agreement had to be negotiated and signed by Israel with most of the Arab Nations. We also believed that the cease-fire agreement alone considerably reduced the risk of hostile action being taken against our Jewish refuge passengers, or our U.S. registered plane and crew.

On the day the cease-fire was supposed to go into effect with Japan at the end of WW II on August 15, 1945, I was on the U.S. Navy plane sent out from Okinawa to buzz (fly low) over every Japanese military installation we could find on the Island of Formosa (now Taiwan) to see if they would shoot at us. I'm very glad to be here to report that there was a lot of fist-shaking displayed, but not one shot was fired at us by the Japanese military and the cease-fire was being honored by the Japanese forces on Formosa.

What we didn't know, as we made our way south from Lydda to Aden, was that the powers that be were developing massive plans to fly Jewish refugees to Israel in numbers never considered, or even thought possible before. It was just by happenstance that our Alaska Airlines plane and crew were the only ones available to actually demonstrate the boundaries of possibilities of what could be done to make the plans for that future operation a success.

Even on the morning of March 11, 1949 as we were making our flight towards Aden, Jewish families were leaving their homes in groups and making their way on foot undaunted by any real or threatened obstacle that might keep them from reaching Israel.

Jewish families from Sa'dah, Kahmr, Sanaa, and others on the high plains had to first climb up and over steep and narrow trails to cross over the high mountains that lay between them and the desert plains that led towards Aden. When the exhausted Yemenite refugees stopped along the mountain trails to rest at night, the wind and the cooler temperatures in the mountains made sleeping almost impossible. Without getting much actual rest during the night, the refugees started the next day almost as tired as when they had stopped.

While crossing the mountains had been difficult and the nights very cold, when they reached the lower desert the sun became hot and the heat and exertion during the day further drained their strength. Daily progress was less than they had planned and what little food and water they had brought with them was running low. They could not continue carrying all of their possessions and had to bury and leave some of them in the desert sand, keeping only what they considered they would need the most.

As they made their way across the desert towards Aden the temperature increased as the elevation of the desert became lower nearer the coast of the Gulf of Aden. With unbelievable fortitude they kept themselves going, never doubting they were destined to make their Aliyah to the Promised Land.

Indeed, most did arrive in the desert sands just east of the Khormaksar RAF Station. Though many had arrived exhausted, ill, thirsty, starved, and penniless, they were there with absolute faith that they would somehow find their way to Israel.

Our single crew and Alaska Airlines DC-4, and the Jewish Yemenite refugees left stranded in Aden, were being brought together as far as we knew, by pure chance. Although I never thought about it at the time, in retrospect, I wonder if destiny might not have played a small role in our being there. Captain Larry Currie and our crew, along with our mechanic Ralph Cheatham, would prove to be quite a team for just such an emergency operation.

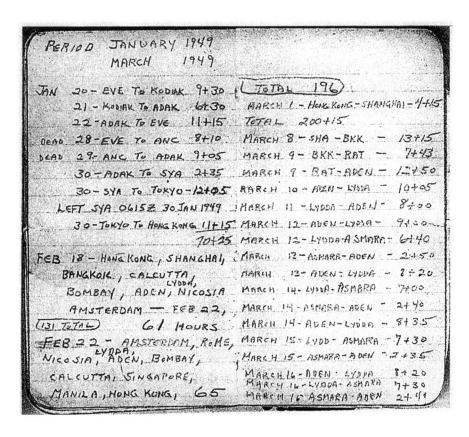

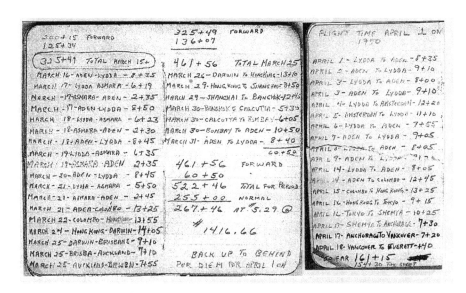

Elgen Long's Personal Log Book from January 20,
through April 18, 1949.

Chapter Four
WITH WINGS AS EAGLES

> *But they that wait upon the Lord shall
> renew their strength; they shall mount
> up with wings as eagles . . .*
>
> **Isaiah 40:31**

It was early Friday afternoon, March 11, 1949 when we parked our DC-4 at Khormaksar RAF Station on our return to Aden direct from Lydda. We knew something special was up when we saw that there was an RAF Officer waiting for Captain Currie on the ramp.

To the best of my knowledge, the Officer introduced himself as Group Captain Keens, Commander of the Khormaksar RAF Station, and handed Captain Currie a cablegram from Alaska Airlines in New York. The cablegram informed us that United States, British, and Israeli interests wanted Alaska Airlines to cooperate with the Aden authorities in flying the Yemenite refugees stranded in Aden to Israel as soon as possible. We understood that to mean we were to do whatever we could to help.

Captain Currie asked RAF Officer Keens how many stranded Yemenite refugees did he have. He answered that he did not have an exact count, but that about 2,000 Yemenites were now living on the desert. They had been able to make it through, before the border was closed between Yemen and the Aden Protectorate. The Officer explained that the Yemenite refugees had arrived by walking, many of them barefoot, over a hundred miles across the mountains and desert from Yemen carrying their children and what few possessions they could with them. They had arrived in Aden with many of them starved, sick, and defenseless. The British had no food to feed them, no medical facilities to treat them, and no place to keep them where they could be protected from the Arab Muslims who considered them the Jewish enemy, and told us that in the Aden Protectorate there had already been more than 80 Jewish people killed by Arab mobs.

He continued to explain, that as we talked, they were sleeping on the desert floor with little food, water, or protection. The sick were suffering in the open without care, and the British Protectorate was barely able to supply them with enough food and water to exist. They had to close the borders to prevent more from coming, but the Aden Protectorate was the refugee's only hope and they are determined to get here at all costs. We could see, it was imperative they be moved to Israel as soon as possible, and RAF Officer Keens emphasized that it was truly a matter of life and death to the refugees.

Keens then asked Captain Currie how many of the refugees did he estimate we could carry from Aden to Lydda on a flight.

Captain Currie answered that we had 48 seats, and children under two years old could sit on a parent's lap. If there were a dozen children under two years of age we could carry maybe 60 people all together, as long as the weight of the passengers and their baggage doesn't overload us. Then Currie asked the Keens how much would he estimate each refugee and their baggage would weigh?

He answered that the Yemenites were small of stature, very thin, and getting thinner. Frankly, many were little more than skin and bones. They have little or no personal effects with them and he would be surprised if the men, women, and children on average weighed more than 80 pounds each. After a pause, Keens added, "Think of these trapped refugees as if they were your own mother, father, wife, or child. What action could you take that would be in the best interest of the refugees to provide help for them?"

Captain Currie then asked me what would be the minimum fuel for a flight from Aden to Lydda with Nicosia as an alternate, if we took-off at 73,000 pounds gross-weight. I answered we would still need 2600 gallons which at the temperature in Aden would weigh about 15,000 pounds. He then asked Ralph what our crew and the engine oil would weigh, and Ralph said about 2,100 pounds.

After a pause and some mental calculations, Captain Currie answered that our plane could carry a maximum payload of 12,000 pounds from Aden to Tel Aviv, but we would need to take-off early in the morning before the temperature got too high. With an average of 80 pounds per person we could carry 150 people, but with only 48 seats, I don't think there would be room for them in the cabin.

Ralph suggested he could take the seats out, and that would provide a lot more space in the cabin for the refugees.

Currie brought up the point that without the seats, the passengers might for some reason all decide to congregate in the rear of the cabin and cause an aircraft out of balance control problem. We had no stewardesses to prevent this or to monitor the refugees, and the DC-4 was already usually a little tail heavy anyway.

Ralph agreed, and suggested he could secure a cargo net across the cabin just aft of the cabin entrance door to block-off the rear of the cabin. The refugees would be instructed that they must not touch, or go behind the net for any reason. Also, he could fill the forward belly cargo with the seats we removed which would move the plane's center of gravity forward.

The RAF Officer answered that he understood the regulatory requirements, but this was truly a matter of life and death for many of these refugees. There was no doubt in his mind that the refugees flying without seats or seat-belts would be much safer than their being forced to stay out on the desert without protection from the Muslims, the elements, adequate medicine, food, or water.

Captain Currie, and the rest of our crew agreed, that the emergency conditions were such we should remove the seats, and see if it was possible to load 150 passengers into a cabin that normally carried only 48.

The RAF Officer said he would arrange to have 150 Yemenite refugees ready for loading onto the plane at 5:00 a.m. the next morning. He then informed us that they would be able to refuel us today, but their aviation fuel was nearly down to their required emergency reserves, and they would have to limit us to a maximum of 400 gallons when we returned from Lydda for the next load of refugees. He then suggested that on our return flight from Lydda we stop in Asmara, Eritrea and refuel before coming back to Aden. They would be able to top-off the fuel load when we arrived in Khormaksar, but only to a maximum of 400 gallons.

Commander RAF Station, Khormaksar, Grp./Capt. L. T. Keens. Photo was taken at the RAF Station, Khormaksar, 1948 Christmas Party.
Photo RAF Photographer Khormaksar
Keith James Collection.

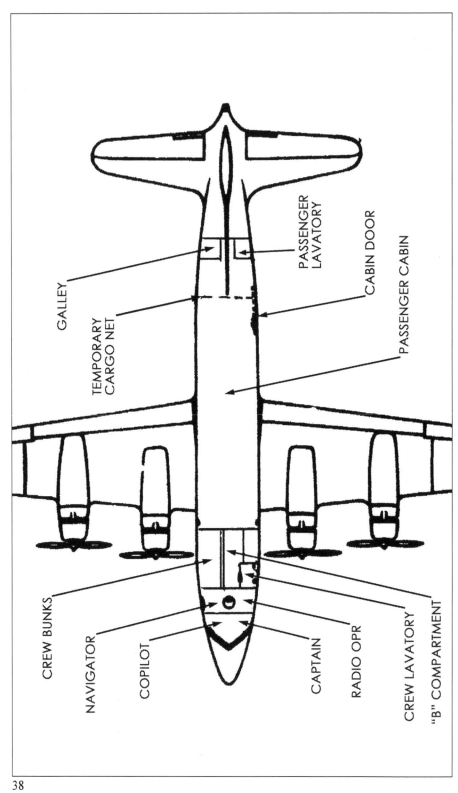

GALLEY

PASSENGER LAVATORY

CABIN DOOR

TEMPORARY CARGO NET

PASSENGER CABIN

CREW BUNKS

NAVIGATOR

COPILOT

CAPTAIN

RADIO OPR

CREW LAVATORY

"B" COMPARTMENT

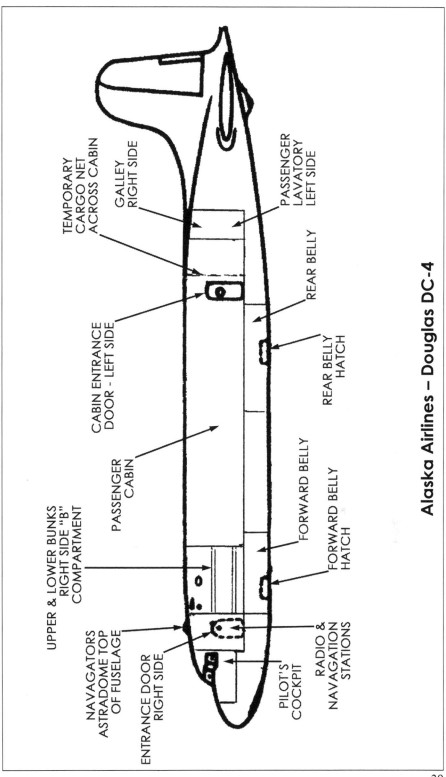

Alaska Airlines – Douglas DC-4

UPPER & LOWER BUNKS RIGHT SIDE "B" COMPARTMENT

TEMPORARY CARGO NET ACROSS CABIN

GALLEY RIGHT SIDE

PASSENGER LAVATORY LEFT SIDE

CABIN ENTRANCE DOOR - LEFT SIDE

REAR BELLY

PASSENGER CABIN

REAR BELLY HATCH

NAVAGATORS ASTRADOME TOP OF FUSELAGE

FORWARD BELLY

ENTRANCE DOOR RIGHT SIDE

FORWARD BELLY HATCH

PILOT'S COCKPIT

RADIO & NAVAGATION STATIONS

Except for Ralph, who had his work cut out for him reconfiguring the cabin plus refueling and all his usual maintenance chores, our crew left the Khormaksar RAF Station for the Crescent Hotel located at the port of Aden.

We actually had the rest of the afternoon off, and after checking in and getting cleaned up in our rooms, we met in the hotel bar for a drink before dinner. As I came into the parlor bar in the lobby I noticed Elliot sitting at a table with an English lady, and a younger woman who looked like she was her daughter. I joined them and found out the ladies were passengers on a ship that had arrived in Aden's harbor. They had come ashore to enjoy the adventure of seeing the sights to be seen in Aden.

The rest of our flight-crew showed up, and our English lady and her daughter had to return to their ship. We finished our drink and went to the dining room to enjoy an early dinner. It was to be the last meal we were to enjoy in a dining room for over a week.

Three comes awfully early in the morning, but I was getting used to putting my feet over the edge of the bed and shoving the covers aside with one hand while fumbling around with the other to find the switch to turn on the bedside lamp. Once upright, the reality of being awake sank in, and I went to the wash basin for a dash of cold water in the face to help me wake up.

A peek out of the curtains to check the weather showed a nearly-full moon in the sky with nary a cloud in sight. No excuses, it was time to go flying again.

We all met in the lobby where they had made a light snack as a substitute for breakfast. After gathering our gear and checking out of the hotel we boarded the crew-bus that would take us to Khormaksar. It left promptly at 4:30 a.m. and wound its way to the airport.

We left the bus at base operations and checked the weather, got our briefing, and filed our flight plan. With the paper work completed, we left the operations office and headed across the ramp to our plane. One glance at the Jewish refugees from Yemen gathered on the ramp near our plane, and we knew from that moment on that there was going to be nothing routine about flying the Jewish Yemenite refugees.

One hundred-fifty men, women, and children were waiting on the ramp; many half-clothed, barefoot, thin, worn, and weary; yet there was an air of excitement that permeated the gathering.

We stopped by RAF Officer Keens, who had spoken with us on our arrival, and there was another RAF Officer standing on the ramp with him. Group Captain Keens introduced his companion as Padre Bennett. It was Saturday

The Harbor at Aden and Khormaksar above Downtown Aden on the Peninsula. Courtesy of Google Maps, ©2015

morning, the Jewish Sabbath day, and we asked the Padre if he knew anything about the Jewish refugees traveling on their Sabbath.

The Padre explained he was just there observing the departure of the Jewish Yemenite refugees. The head Rabbi in Tel Aviv, Israel had been contacted and cleared them to travel because it was a matter of life and death. It would be alright for them to travel on the Sabbath.

Yemenites on the ramp at Khormaksar for flight to Lydda, Isreal.
Photo by Kluger Zoltan; Courtesy of Israeli National Photo Archive

We noticed many of the passengers were gathered around one man who was talking to them. Group Captain Keens, explained that most of our passengers had never seen an airplane before, and didn't have any idea how it operated or how it was able to fly like a bird. He pointed to the man that was talking to them and explained that he was their spiritual leader. He was trying to explain to the refugees that they were to enter the airplane, and it would fly them to Israel. They did not understand how that could be. The man reminded them of the scripture that told them that when the time of Redemption came the Lord shall renew their strength; and it was prophesized that they shall mount up with wings as eagles.

The refugees knew the scripture, and that gave them the courage to climb up the metal ladder one-by-one, and enter into the aircraft's cabin. That there weren't any seats in the plane's cabin would mean nothing to them. The Yemenites did not sit in chairs like Europeans; they had always sat on their haunches or just on the floor, and so they did after entering the plane. We really never believed that we would be able to get all 150 into the DC-4's cabin, but sure enough a young man was the last one to be squeezed in, and the cabin door was shut behind him.

Captain Currie asked Group Commander Keens about the men of military age being on the flight, and the answer was that because the war had ended the day before, he didn't believe it was applicable anymore.

We were ready to go, and went forward on the other side of the plane to enter the cockpit through the crew entrance door at the navigator's station. As soon as Ralph had pulled the gear pins and was on board, we closed the cockpit door and when they got the all-engines-clear signal from the fire-guard on the ground the pilots started the engines. None of us had ever heard of so many people flying in a DC-4 before, and as far as we knew it was going to be a first for everyone on board.

System checks, engine run-ups, and everything completed we were cleared for take-off from Aden right on our planned time of 6:00 a.m. Saturday, March 12, 1949, for our first flight of Jewish Yemenite refugees to Israel. We could only imagine the emotions that our passengers must have felt as we made the take-off, and banked in our turn out over the Gulf of Aden heading towards Perim Island and the southern entrance to the Red Sea. To our passengers, it must have been nothing short of absolutely amazing to actually be in flight like an eagle in the sky.

While the actual flight was normal to us, it must have seemed every bit like the prophesized miracle of the Great Redemption to our Yemenite refugee passengers, whose families had been waiting through a hundred generations for their return to the Holy Land and the new Jewish state of Israel.

There were no surprises or special problems that occurred during our flight and when Elliot was asked to check with Lydda Radio, he got a single letter "P" as an answer which signaled we were cleared to proceed on into Lydda.

Captain Currie made a smooth landing, and our passengers were relatively quiet compared to the loud cheers we had heard on previous arrivals from our Shanghai and European refugees. I believe, to our Yemenite passengers, the flight was more of a religious event than a social one. However, many raised their face to the sky when they reached the bottom of the ladder and touched Israeli soil for the first time. That gesture was as a prayer of thanks for their deliverance. The arrival was a moving moment for our passengers and for us. Without anyone saying a word, I really felt again like it was a good thing we had done.

We still had no knowledge of what was to come in the near future. At that moment we were only thinking about, refueling and getting airborne for our first trip to Asmara, Eritrea. None of us had ever been to Eritrea, but we had heard that Italy had wrested it from Ethiopia in two wars and it was an Italian colony before WW II. The allied forces had defeated the Italian Forces in 1941 during WW II, and the British were still administering Eritrea in 1949.

Our passengers had been cleared, and the cabin was cleaned and disinfected by the airport personnel, while Ralph refueled the plane. We completed our flight plan, filed VFR for Asmara, and were airborne from Lydda for Asmara before 4:00 p.m. local time. It would be after sunset when we arrived at Asmara, but there would be almost a full moon shining by the time we arrived.

Our route was the same as when we were flying to Aden until we reached 39 degrees East Longitude, which was about 400 miles, or about two hours of flying due north of Asmara. At that point we would track due south on 39 degrees East Longitude to cross the northern coast of Eritrea, well south of the Eritrean-Sudanese border, and on track direct to Asmara.

The pilots could navigate themselves from Lydda to Beersheba and down to Eilat (formerly Umm-Rashrash) at the Gulf of Aqaba. From there I gave them the heading to fly down the middle of the Gulf of Aqaba to the Red Sea and the heading to go down the middle of the Red Sea towards Perim Island, and asked them to wake me an hour after we had turned to enter the Red Sea.

Co-pilot Lester was already asleep in the lower bunk, as I crawled into the upper bunk shortly after take-off for three or four hours of sleep.

Elliot woke me up, and as I crawled out of the bunk, I noticed Captain Currie had already replaced Lester in the lower bunk. I told Elliot I would monitor the radio for him if he wanted to get some sleep. He started taking off his shoes without hesitation.

It was dark outside, and I looked up into the astrodome to confirm that the stars were visible, and as usual the sky above was clear. I checked the compass heading that the pilots were flying and it was exactly what I had given them. Bill was in the left seat. He said they had entered into the Red Sea an hour before, and had been holding the prescribed heading since then. Captain Currie wanted to get up an hour before we were due to arrive in Asmara.

The nearly-full moon was up, and Bill said they hadn't seen any glow of lights from the shore on either side. All had been smooth and normal as we flew southward down the middle of the Red Sea.

I closed the curtain between the pilots and the navigation station, and turned on the lights at my navigation table to calculate the celestial observations of stars that would give me a course, and a speed check of our progress. All together it took nearly 30 minutes to take observations the stars, calculate the fix, and plot it on the chart. The star fix showed us about 300 miles south of the Sinai

Peninsula and on course in the middle of the Red Sea. We were about halfway to Asmara, and should intercept 39 degrees East Longitude in about another hour.

I had Elliot's headphones on and was monitoring the en route frequency, but there were no calls or signals that were directed to us from any of the stations on the frequency. We were still over three hours from Asmara, and I would take another fix in about a half-hour; well before our course would intercept 39 degrees East Longitude.

The next star fix confirmed our position as we progressed down the Red Sea. I measured the distance to 39 degrees East Longitude, and I calculated we should turn at 8:30 p.m. local time to fly due south down 39 degrees East Longitude. We would arrive at Asmara at about 10:30 p.m. and should wake Captain Currie at 9:30.

As we flew south down 39 degrees east, we could barely see the glow from the lights of Port Sudan off in the distance to our right, and with the moonlight we had no trouble seeing the shore line when we crossed into Eritrea. Captain Currie was awakened at 9:30 p.m., and sat down in the co-pilots seat. Lester was to stay in the left-seat and make the landing at Asmara.

The Asmara Airport was located just northeast of the city of Asmara and was situated on a high plateau over 7600 feet above sea level. We were flying at

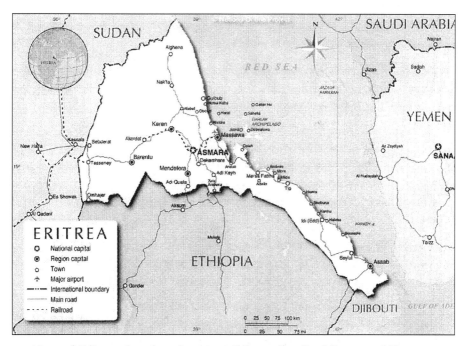

Map of Eritrea showing Asmara, Eritrea, the Red Sea, and Yemen.
Map Courtesy www.nationsonline.org

an altitude of 9,500 feet, which was high enough to clear the terrain that rose rapidly between the coast and the airport.

Asmara had a population of around 100,000 people, and the lights of the city were easy to see as we approached from the north. We spotted the airport-beacon light a little away from the city, and aimed directly for the airport. The pilots contacted the tower on VHF and got the altimeter setting, wind and weather, and the number of the runway in use as we approached the airport.

We made a left hand pattern around the airport, and put the gear-down on the downwind leg and lowered the flaps to 15 degrees, then on base leg the flaps were put down to 35 degrees. As he turned onto final to line up with the runway, Bill Lester slowed the plane to final approach speed as he descended to touchdown a few hundred feet down the runway. Bill made the landing and he did a very good job of it.

As the plane slowed after landing and was ready to turn off the runway, the tower began directing us to the gas pit for refueling. As we turned onto a taxiway that was taking us towards the parking ramp our landing lights illuminated a Curtiss C-46 aircraft parked there. As we got closer, and the light became brighter, we could see its' nose was sticking up into the air and the fuselage was broken and bent just aft of the wing. Then Captain Currie asked Bill to stop, and I heard him say, "That's an Alaska Airlines C-46. What the hell is it doing here in Asmara?"

We had no idea there was another Alaska Airlines airplane within 5,000 miles of Asmara. We started taxiing again towards the gas pit, and all of us were astonished that the plane was there, and obviously had been damaged somehow.

We were guided into our parking spot by the gas man with lighted signaling-wands for refueling, and after we had come to a stop the pilots shut down the engines. Ralph opened the crew door, and the gas man put a ladder up to the door for us to use to exit. The first question asked when we got off the plane was about the Alaska Airlines C-46 we had seen on the ramp.

It seems that several weeks earlier the two-engine C-46 had a failure of one of its engines just after taking-off. As it was coming around to land on the one remaining engine, the plane's tail wheel had hit the top of a bank just short of the runway, and it caused the fuselage to be badly bent during the landing. We learned that no one was seriously injured though the airplane's fuselage was damaged beyond repair.

Captain Currie asked the gas man what the C-46 was doing here in Asmara. He said he didn't know, but the plane had been full of drums of aviation gasoline that it was taking to Aden when it had lost the engine. He believed that some of the mechanics were still in Asmara, and would come out most days to salvage what they could from the wrecked plane. Ralph had installed the gear pins, and checked that the fuel man had put the wheel-chocks in place, before working with the gas man to refuel us to 2900 gallons. As soon I had finished calculating the flight plan of a little over two hours and 30 minutes to Aden, I headed to a bunk for a little sleep. It had been a long day, and tomorrow was going to be another one. I thought I'd better sleep while I could.

All I had was a short nap, and woke up and went to the navigation table when they started the engines. Our landing lights again illuminated the damaged Alaska Airlines C-46 as we taxied past it on our way to the runway for take-off. It was after midnight when we were airborne and turned to head for the coast of the Red Sea and Perim Island. We soon leveled off at 9,500 feet and headed eastward across Eritrea for the western shore of the Red Sea.

It didn't take long before the plateau abruptly dropped several thousand feet to the lower terrain near the shoreline of the Red Sea. We passed to the south of Massawa, which if my memory of geography is correct, was considered at onetime to have the hottest temperatures of any place on earth. When we were over the coast we headed direct to Perim Island at the southern end of the Red Sea. After Perim Island we followed offshore with the Yemen coastline on our left until we reached Aden and the Khormaksar RAF Station.

It was nearly 4:00 a.m. local time when we landed at Khormaksar on Sunday morning, March 13, 1949. We had logged 18.5 hours of flying in the 22 hours since we had left at 6:00 a.m. the day before. As we climbed down the ladder to the ramp Group Commander Keens was there again to greet us. He told us that the next load of 150 refugees would be arriving momentarily, and the fuel truck could supply us with up to 400 gallons of fuel if necessary.

Strange as it may seem, not one of us even thought we should make a complaint of our taking-off again in two hours for Lydda. It was not a complaint, but a practical suggestion from Elliot that he was not really needed on the flight, and as I was also a radio-operator and could handle any communications that might become necessary, Judd volunteered to just stay in Aden and leave more time open in the crew bunks for everyone else.

Captain Currie approved of his staying in Aden, and immediately the RAF Officer asked if he should get two more refugees to replace his weight. Currie politely said that the 150 Yemenite refugees in the cabin had proved to be the right number and should stay unchanged.

Another report came from our mechanic Ralph. He had completed his preflight, and there wasn't a single hydraulic, oil, or air leak anywhere on the plane. There was not one thing on the plane that needed to be written up in the logbook, or that needed to be repaired. As far as he was concerned, when the fuel and oil tanks were filled to the right level, he was ready to go.

The ramp was still being lit a little by moon-light when the trucks began arriving with the refugees for our flight. They soon began moving the passengers up the ladder and into the aircraft's cabin. Their spiritual advisor was now more experienced with the process of loading the refugees and it was progressing with noticeably less difficulty or resistance. As before, the refugees were a sad sight to see. I wondered again, how they could continue to persevere.

We walked to the operations office to get the weather and file our flight plan. The upper winds at our flight level were not as strong as they had been the day before, and it was only going to take us a little over eight hours to fly to Lydda today. We were going to leave again at 6:00 a.m. local time, and I headed for a bunk. The pilots knew their way to Perim Island and I gave them the heading to fly from Perim Island up the middle of the Red Sea. Unless they needed me I would try to sleep until we were an hour north of Perim Island. As it turned out I had no trouble at all sleeping for nearly three hours till then. When Ralph did wake me, Captain Currie was already asleep in the bunk below. As soon as I slipped out of the bunk, Ralph climbed in. It never had a chance to even get cool.

The first thing I did was use the drift-meter to take a drift-sight and adjust the compass heading the pilot was maintaining a couple degrees to the left of the compass course to keep us flying up the middle of the Red sea. The visibility was good and as long as we could not see either shore we were quite confident no one had an accurate knowledge of where we were.

Every hour I would take a drift sight and adjust our compass heading as needed, and waited to take a noon fix on the sun. As long as we left Aden anywhere near 6:00 a.m. the noon fix would be about an hour before we reached the Gulf of Aqaba.

With Ralph and Currie asleep in the bunks, I left the cockpit to go back to the passenger cabin to take a check on the passengers, and make sure everything was alright. I came back into the cockpit about ten minutes later shaking my head. One of the passengers had lit up a gas stove in the middle of the cabin to boil water for tea. I got the gas stove shut- off, and with head-shaking and hand-signals got them to understand that they were not to light up any stoves again. I couldn't help but laugh as they had no way to know of the danger that the flame of the gas stoves could be in an airplane.

When I took my local apparent noon fix of the sun, and it showed us to be on course and on flight plan as we approached the northern end of the Red Sea and the mouth of the Gulf of Aqaba.

Captain Currie was awakened as we approached the Sinai Peninsula, and Bill headed for the lower bunk. At Captain Curries' request, I contacted Lydda Radio and got a one letter answer this time of "W;" it was all-clear for us to continue on to Lydda.

Even though the flight was already becoming routine, we felt a great sense of accomplishment in being able to successfully remove so many refugees from the terrible situation they had found themselves in Aden, and deliver them to the land they had dreamed of returning to for generations.

We landed at Lydda a little after 2:00 p.m. local time, Sunday, March 13, 1949. There were many more people gathered at the airport when we landed at Lydda this time than there had been on our first arrival. Though no press releases of our flights had been made, and it was not reported in the newspapers or on the radio, it seemed word of our flights had somehow reached many people who wanted to personally witness the off-loading of the Yemenites as they arrived in Israel. To the crowd of spectators at the event it must have seemed a special spiritual moment of great importance as the refugees, after waiting thousands of years, climbed down the ladder and for the first time touched the soil of their biblically prophesized "Promised Land."

There were no press or photographers to catch the moment when these early Jewish Yemenites actually lived the biblical dream they had waited thousands of years for. It was a personal moment between them and their beliefs and faith.

The 12 early flights we made in March and April of 1949 were to rescue the Jewish Yemenites from a life-threatening situation they faced on the desert outskirts of Aden. Unlike the later Yemenite refugees that were received at Camp Hashed, that had been washed, doctored, fed, and clothed before their flights on Operation Magic Carpet to Israel. Our passengers were brought directly from the desert near Aden and boarded onto our DC-4 aircraft every morning still un-washed, un-doctored, and partially un-clothed. It was to be another three months before Israel would be able to get Camp Hashed operational in the Aden.

Later, during Operation Magic Carpet, the Yemenite Refugees were healthy and clean, wearing clothes and shoes that were provided for them at Hashed. Unfortunately though, many of the early Yemenite refugees may have arrived in Lydda as they had left the Aden desert barefoot, sparsely clothed, sick and undernourished. They arrived with the obvious dignity of having lived a millenniums-old prophecy and had waited more than a hundred-lifetimes to come true for them.

Our flight-crew was composed of relatively young men trained in the disciplines of aviation, with little or no background in international politics or government operations. We felt good about doing the best job we could, under very difficult circumstances, to assist people in making their lives better. What we did not realize was that we were just a small, though vital, part of a much larger effort of many people around the world that were working diligently to make it all possible.

The plight of hundreds of thousands of displaced people all over the world was recognized by governments, international organizations, and ethnic societies. A world-wide effort to bring aid to help correct the situation was already in progress. Captain Currie and our crew had no knowledge that we were part of this process. Many organizations were watching the successes, failures, and progress that the Alaska Airlines refugee flights were making as they searched for the best way to organize future flights. In the coming months, they would have to handle the tens of thousands of refugees that would be leaving their present homes of refuge for Israel.

James Wooten, President of Alaska Airlines, was in contact with The American Jewish Joint Distribution Committee in New York.

In Washington D.C., Former Secretary of the U. S. Treasury, Henry Morgenthau Jr., whose father was the U. S. Ambassador to the Ottoman Empire, Henry Morgenthau Sr., that the Jews had asked for help nearly 35 years earlier. Now his son was heading a nationwide effort to raise $250,000,000 to finance future refugee relief and relocation projects.

A joint Congressional resolution of Congress authorized the United States to contribute $16,000,000 to the United Nations General Assembly toward the relief of 700,000 refugees of the recent fighting in Israel, and President Truman was about to sign the Congressional resolution with "Gratification." In a formal statement, the President expressed his hope that a permanent solution of the Middle East refugee problem would be found before the relief program was ended.

Back in New York, Mr. Irving M. Engel, Chairman of the executive committee of The American Jewish Committee, and Maj. General Carl A. Hardigg, chief of the supply and transport division of the International Refugee Organization, were making plans for a trip to Israel. They were going to Israel to study the physical and economic conditions as it pertained to the nation's ability to absorb some 150,000 immigrants over the next eight months.

Unbeknownst to our flight crew, all of this was happening as we off-loaded our second load of Yemenite refugee passengers in Lydda.

We took-off from Lydda for Asmara shortly after the cabin was serviced and disinfected, and the plane was refueled. The trip to Asmara was about the same as it had been the night before. On our arrival, we were pleased to find that the Asmara Operations Officer was indeed good to his word and had contacted the Alaska Airlines' mechanics, and one was there to meet us. After greetings, Bill Lester and I went to check the latest weather and to file our flight plan at operations, while Ralph fueled the plane. Captain Currie and the Alaska Airlines' mechanic conversed about what each of them were doing in Asmara, and what had happened to the crashed Alaska Airlines C-46.

There had been two Alaska Airlines C-46s, N1240N and N1241N that were flown from the U.S. to Lydda across the Atlantic to fly refugees out of Aden to Lydda. As close as could be determined, Captain Warren Metzger flying C-46 N1240N made two flights from Aden to Lydda with approximately 65 Jewish Yemenite refugee passengers on each flight. However, because the C-46s proved to be unable to carry enough fuel in the planes normal fuel tanks to safely make the Aden to Lydda flight, the company assigned them to fly out of Asmara and Nicosia carrying loads of aviation gas in fuel drums to resupply Aden and Lydda with fuel for the two Alaska Airlines DC-4s.

The two Alaska Airlines DC-4s, NC90915 and NC66756, had arrived in Lydda in early January 1949. They had been sent to fly Jewish refugees to Lydda, and were flown by Captain Robert Maguire and Captain Sam Silver. During a flight on February 8, 1949, DC-4 NC66756 had a failure of number two engine while flying out of Asmara, and returned to land back at Asmara.

Before the operation of the two DC-4s ended their refugee operations in Israel and returned to the U.S. for cabin seating modifications and certification on February 19, 1949, they were reported to have made at least 5 trips with Jewish Yemenite refugees from Aden to Lydda. They are estimated to have carried approximately 110 refugees on each of their flights and are estimated to have flown a total of 550 Jewish Yemenites from Aden to Israel in January and early February of 1949.

Though no records of the flights have been located, it is known that the Alaska Airlines DC-4s had also flown flights of Jewish Syrian refugees to Lydda in early 1949, as part of what was later to become known as "Operation Ezra."

On January 21, 1949, the crash of the C-46, N1241N, ended its participation in making flights.

As close as can be determined the C-46, N1640N, under the command of Captain Warren Metzger had flown approximately 130 Jewish Yemenite refugees from Aden to Israel, and Captains Maguire and Silver approximately 550 on the DC-4's. The four-plane operation by Alaska Airlines had lasted from January 4, 1949 to February 18, 1949. During those 45 days, the four airplanes and their four crews had managed to fly a total of approximately 680 of the Jewish Yemenite refugees from their precarious position in Aden to the new homeland in Israel.

The known reports indicate that there were no further Jewish Yemenite refugee flights made by Alaska Airlines after February 18, 1949, until Captain Currie and his crew made their first Aden to Lydda Yemenite refugee flight on March 12, 1949.

Unfortunately, because of the unavailability of aviation fuel at both Aden and Lydda, along with the less than optimum aircraft cabin-configuration and insufficient C-46 fuel capacity, the flights proved to be less than an operational or financial success. For the operations to become efficient there was going to have to be modifications to the aircraft as well as changes to how they were operated, refueled, and maintained.

When Alaska Airlines' President, James Wooten returned to New York, he reported the results of the operation to Alaska Airlines' Chairman of the Board, Raymond Marshall. Unfortunately, after the bill for the fuel used on the flights was paid, and the money Wooten had borrowed was repaid, the money paid by the JDC in Paris for the refugees flown was not enough to cover the operations expenses. It was said that in April of 1949, Wooten had offered his resignation to Mr. Marshall.

Mr. Wooten also reported to the JDC in New York of the problems the Yemenite refugee flights had encountered, and discussed with them a proposal of how a much more efficient and productive operation could be conducted with Alaska Airlines DC-4 aircraft equipped and certified with passenger seating for 120 passengers, and flight operations specifically designed to fly refugees economically. While no decision on his proposal was reached, it was listened to and discussed with serious interest.

Alaska President, James Wooten, then went to the Jewish Joint Distribution Committee's European Headquarters in Paris to meet the JDC's European and North African Director, Joseph Swartz, to discuss an arrangement wherein James Wooten proposed an Alaska Airlines contract designed specifically to fly the tens-of-thousands of Yemenite refugees from Aden, as well as the thousands of other Jewish refugees from Europe, Asia, and Africa as part of the coming great movement of refugees to Israel.

It is possible Wooten was able to point out to Mr. Swartz, a demonstration by a single Alaska Airlines DC-4 and crew that had been operating a DC-4 as he envisioned the future contract would be operated. The single DC-4, with one crew flying it, had been able to fly 1800 Jewish Yemenite refugees from Aden to Lydda in only 29 days.

Captain Currie and his crew, in seven days, Saturday, March 12 thru March 18, 1949, had made seven Aden to Lydda roundtrips flying a total of approximately 1,050 Yemenite Refugees to Israel. This was the kind of operation that was possible with Alaska Airlines DC-4s and crews in the future when they were operated as Wooten was proposing to the JDC they would be.

In seven days, they had flown over 126 hours and averaged over 18 hours a day flying the Yemenite refugees. If they had kept that up they would fly 6,593 hours in a year; 6,593 hours is more flying than the average pilot in the world does in a lifetime. However, an operation staffed with proper crew and maintenance personnel was only requiring the DC-4 to do exactly what it was designed for and capable of accomplishing.

When discussed later, by people in Alaska Airlines who knew of the flights, they described Captain Currie and his crew as iron-men having literally lived on the airplane for a week, never landing except to reload or refuel. Significantly, no mention was ever made that the DC-4 was doing anything out of the ordinary, because in reality it was just doing what it was designed for.

It had been a very memorable "week that was," however we didn't keep it up. We took a day off on Saturday, March 19, 1949, but on the next day, Sunday, March 20th we took-off again from Aden for Lydda on our eighth trip with 150 more Yemenite Refugees. When we arrived in Lydda, there was a cablegram for Captain Currie from Alaska Airlines in New York.

The cablegram instructed us to get legal rest in Tel Aviv, add our Alaska Airlines' stewardesses back onto our crew, and fly via Aden to Hong Kong as soon as possible. So after making sure the plane was serviced and arrangements made for the seats to be put back into the cabin, we left Ralph to finish the maintenance, and headed for the hotel in Tel Aviv to sleep in a real bed for the second night in a row. We had an early dinner and headed for bed before dark. The wake-up call was for midnight, and we hoped to take-off from Lydda before 3:00 a.m. local time.

We gathered in the lobby before 1:00 a.m., but as there was no breakfast available at the hotel we went back to our rooms to collect our suitcases and left for the airport. When we arrived at the Lydda terminal building we were met by our stewardesses who were already there. They were to see about the catering for the flight and check out the cabin galley since it had been blocked off since we started flying the Yemenite refugees.

The winds aloft hadn't changed much since we had flown up from Aden yesterday, and the weather was good all the way to Asmara and Aden. After we got our flight plan to Asmara filed we went out to the plane and started our pre-flight checks. The stewardesses had been informed there would be a few Israeli passengers going as far as Aden with us, and there would be catering of snacks provided for the passengers and the crew. Some Israeli men were the passengers, and they came onboard soon after we had arrived at the plane.

We took-off from Lydda before 3:00 a.m. Monday, March 21, 1949, and estimated the flight to Asmara would take us less than six hours. It was daylight when we arrived in Asmara, and we were on the ground less than an hour-and-a-half when we were able to take-off for Aden.

It was the first time we had made a daylight flight out of Asmara, and we were amazed to see how abruptly the high plateau on which Asmara was situated dropped away thousands of feet to almost sea level as we headed for Aden via Perim Island.

The time was near 1:00 p.m. in the afternoon when we arrived at Khormaksar marking the completion of eight roundtrips of Yemenite refugees to Lydda in nine days, and had flown somewhere near 1200 Yemenites home to Israel in the process. According to what the RAF Officer had told us earlier, there must still be nearly 800 hundred more waiting for a flight. We could only hope that good care would be provided for them until they could be flown to Israel.

When we checked in at the RAF operations office there was a cablegram from Alaska Airlines in New York for Captain Currie. It directed us to fly from Aden to Hong Kong as soon as possible with our full-crew, mechanic, and stewardesses. Elliot had been notified, and was on his way from the hotel.

Without passengers, the quickest way to Hong Kong was to fly nonstop from Aden to Colombo, and then nonstop from Colombo to Hong Kong. With the light-winds from the east, it was going to take us about 13-and-a-half-hours to Ratmalana, and Ralph was to fuel the plane to 3100 gallons for the flight. That meant he would have to fill all of the six wing tanks plus put some 230 gallons in the fuselage tank. Without question or comment, the RAF was willing to provide us with whatever gas we needed.

We would be taking off about 4:00 p.m. and the temperature would be high, but with no payload on the plane we would get off easily with only the approximate 18,600 pounds of fuel on board. We filed an Instrument flight plan, direct from Khormaksar to Ratmalana at an altitude of 9,000 feet. With everyone on board a U.S. citizen, flying in a U.S. plane, we were nearly back to standard flight operating procedures.

Our departure from Aden for Colombo was near 5:00 p.m. and it was going to be nearly an all night-time flight. I took a three-star fix about two hours after we had leveled-off at 9,000 feet to check that our compass heading was taking us on our desired course to Colombo. The air was smooth, the stars were bright and the fix showed we were making good our course and expected groundspeed towards the RAF Base at Ratmalana. I gave Elliot two position reports ahead of time, and as there were empty seats in the cabin, I could grab an available bunk or seat for two hours of sleep between fixes. Our faithful DC-4 made the flight with ease, and we arrived at Ratmalana after a flight of about 13-and-a-half hours. It was already daylight in Colombo, Ceylon (Sri Lanka) when we landed about 8:00 a.m. local time Tuesday, March 22, 1949.

After mentioning our previous experience with palm trees, Captain Currie didn't want to take-off for Hong Kong with the temperatures as high as it was, and didn't want to land in Hong Kong till daylight. We would delay our flight to Hong Kong till 9:00 p.m. that evening and take 12 hours of rest.

The crew bus took us to a lovely Victorian era hotel located just a few miles south of the Ratmalana RAF Base on a beautiful beach at Dehiwala-Mount Lavinia. The hotel was named the Mount Lavinia, and was a gem of gems to our tired eyes and bodies. We couldn't help ourselves, and within an hour after our arrival we were body boarding in the beautiful waters along the beach and soaking in the warm sunlight.

Unfortunately, I really bruised the inside of my right thigh when the nose of the board dug into the sand as I came into an area of shallow water at high speed. Luckily, there was no bleeding from the area just a bad bruise that was going to be sore for a few days.

I was hoping we would be heading for home before too long, and bought a Deep Blue Star Sapphire gem for my wife that I could have made into a ring. The price seemed to me much less than I had ever heard of in the United States, and appeared of good color and quality.

We returned to our rooms from the beach after making a stop on the hotel patio on our way back to watch a snake charmer do his thing. He played his flute like instrument they call a pungi, and a cobra came out of its' basket and swayed in rhythm with the music the charmer was playing. I was to learn later that the cobra was really following the pungi instrument back and forth as the charmer swayed it with the rhythm of the music. The cobra saw the pungi instrument as a threat and followed its' every move to be ready to strike to defend itself. It was something this small town boy from Oregon had never had the opportunity to see before.

A shower and shave before lunch, and service in the dining room that was not only unusual, but a treat of treats in its grand-manner and general excellence. It was the first time I can remember of having ever been served in the grand-manner of the days of Queen Victoria. After lunch was over I really didn't want to leave the dining room, but our wake-up call was for 6:00 p.m. and five hours of sound sleep in a comfortable and quiet bed was sorely needed.

We left the Mount Lavinia Hotel at 7:00 p.m. for the Ratmalana RAF aerodrome. I already had made up the flight plan and it only took about 15 minutes to do the calculations when I got the winds-aloft at the weather and operations office. We filed an instrument flight-plan from Colombo direct to Hong Kong, and were airborne with plenty of clearance over the palm trees before 9:00 p.m. local time. The flight went as planned and we arrived at the Wagland Island radio-beacon just off the south coast of Hong Kong's Victoria Island after 10:00 a.m. local time. There were clouds in the area and we let down in a rectangular box around the Wagland Island radio-beacon till we broke-out into the clear below all the clouds, and could proceed visually through Lyman Gap into Hong Kong Harbor to land at the Kai Tak Airport. It was just a little before 11:00 a.m. local time Wednesday morning, March 23, 1949 when we parked our DC-4 and shut-down its engines at Hong Kong.

There was a cablegram from Alaska Airlines for Captain Currie. We were to depart at 6:00 a.m. the next morning with a ship's crew of 40 passengers to Auckland, New Zealand, and return to Hong Kong with a returning ship's crew, as soon as possible for another flight. Our two stewardesses and Ralph Cheatham were to stay in Hong Kong and flight mechanic, J. Vince Weipert was to join our crew to replace Ralph.

The Peninsula Hotel was elegant and its food was great, but we had been absolutely spoiled by the service at the Mount Lavinia Hotel in Ceylon. After dinner some of the crew went to have a night cap at the bar, but I voted for nine hours of sleep before the 4:00 a.m. wake-up call.

What we didn't know was that the trip to New Zealand was only going to be a short, very busy, and very interesting three-day hiatus, before we would be right back doing what we could to help relocate some of the world's refugees.

Snake charmer with cobras.

Chapter Five
ALASKA AIRLINES DOWN UNDER

Early the next morning our passengers were onboard, and we had filed a fourteen-hour instrument flight plan from Hong Kong non-stop direct to Darwin, Australia.

We were airborne just after 6:00 a.m. Thursday morning, March 24, 1949, with just enough light to clearly see our way through Lyman Gap out to the open South China Sea, as we made our way to our cruising altitude of 9,000 feet.

Soon after we had reached 9,000 feet and had adjusted our engines for cruising, Bill Lester asked Elliot if it was okay for him to turn on the Bendix command-radio that the pilots used to contact the Alaska Airlines Radio in Alaska when using the radiotelephone for voice communications. Elliot said it was okay with him, but Alaska was 5,000 miles away and he didn't think they would get through to them.

Bill tried a call anyway, and to every one's surprise Alaska Airlines Radio in Anchorage answered with a voice signal that was loud and clear. Bill made a personal greeting to them and told Anchorage we had just left Hong Kong en route to Darwin, Australia. Anchorage was also surprised how loud and clear the signal from our plane was, and said they would relay our departure message to the company offices.

Fourteen hours is a long flight, but it was interesting to us as we flew over areas we had never flown before. From the South China Sea, we crossed Palawan Island and into the Sulu Sea then across the Sulu Archipelago into the Celebes Sea to the Celebes Islands. All exotic names of exotic places we never dreamed we would ever actually see. Just for a little extra drama we held a Davey Jones initiation event for those "Pollywogs" amongst us who had never crossed the equator before.

A little cold water poured over their head had to suffice for the usual full dunking a pollywog would get on a ship. At least we had upheld the traditional ceremony for initiating a new "Shellback" as they crossed the equator for the first time.

About three hours after crossing the equator we landed at Darwin, Australia at about 9:00 p.m. local time. None of us had ever landed at the Darwin Airport before, and there was a large hump that rose between one-end of the runway and the other. It was unusual to land and only see part of the runway before you, as the far end was below the rise in the middle. It was a good long runway, but you couldn't tell it by looking out the cockpit window.

We parked at the terminal building and James began fueling as soon as the gas truck arrived. Captain Currie and I went to the meteorological office to get the winds and weather for our next leg to Brisbane, Australia. The weather was good and our flight plan calculated it would take just under nine hours to fly to Brisbane, and we filed an instrument flight plan at 9,000 feet. The fuel required en route was 1870 U.S. gallons and Captain Currie added a reserve of 530 gallons. I went out to the plane to tell Vince Weipert to fuel to 2400.

In many locations, the fuel was not delivered in U.S. Gallons. In those places Vince had to make sure the conversion was accurate, and we were delivered 3.79 liters for every U.S. gallon required. Just to further complicate it a bit more, some places measured fuel by Imperial gallons which were equal to 4.55 liters or 1.2 U.S. gallons. The saving grace was our fuel gauges in the cockpit and the fuel dip sticks always read in U.S. gallons. That is what the pilots and flight mechanic checked to confirm the fuel on board before we started engines.

As we were getting ready to depart from Darwin, Australia, we had no knowledge of what was going on at the same time on the other side of the world in New York City. The Holland-America Liner Nieuw Amsterdam was getting ready to depart New York for English Channel ports and Rotterdam, Netherlands, with 1120 passengers.

Four of the passengers on the Nieuw Amsterdam were Mr. Irving M. Engel, Chairman of the Executive Committee of the American Jewish Joint Distribution Committee, accompanied by his wife, Katherine, and Major General Carl A. Hardigg, Chief of the supply and transport division of the International Refugee Organization, with his wife, Mary. They were traveling to Israel to determine if the newly formed nation had the capability to absorb about 150,000 immigrants in the coming year. They would also be touring Western Europe and North Africa to determine the condition of Jews located in those areas.

It might be said, they were to determine the pace that they believed refugees arriving in Israel could be accommodated, and then strike a balance with the ability of aircraft to deliver them. Mr. Engel concentrated on the physical and economic capabilities, while General Hardigg focused on his specialty, transportation and supply.

In Darwin, the Alaska Airlines plane's passenger cabin and lavatories had been cleaned, and in a little over an hour the galleys were replenished with food and supplies for the flight to Brisbane. The ramp service was completed by 11:00 p.m., but the gas truck ran out of fuel and had to go back to get replenished before we could have the required 2400 gallons.

The gas truck was gone for nearly an hour before it returned, and Vince could finish the fueling. We were able to reload our passengers about midnight. It was after midnight when we took-off using the same runway we had landed on. Again, we could not see the other end until we were half-way down the runway. It was Friday morning, March 25, 1949 when we left Darwin.

We leveled off at 9,000 feet, and there were many Australian stations along our route that the pilot could contact by VHF radiotelephone to make our progress reports. The pilots agreed to handle the communications en route to Brisbane. Bill pointed out to me that our route from Darwin to Brisbane took us over Australia's Northern Territory and Queensland, and that Qantas Airlines had started their airline there. What I had never realized before, was that the name of Australia's major airline, "QANTAS," was actually an acronym for Queensland and Northern Territories Air Services.

With the pilots making our progress reports there was no need for Elliot to stand a constant CW telegraph watch so he took to the upper bunk. Before he left, I asked him if I could use his amateur call sign to see what amateur radio was like in Australia. He said to go ahead and use it.

I sat down in the radio operator's seat and tuned the ART-13 Transmitter to about 14,250 kilocycles (kilocycles are now called kilohertz) on the radio amateur's 20-meter band. I selected to transmit on voice and gave a general call of "CQ" for anyone to answer just to see if any Australian amateurs were up and on the air at this time of the morning. An Australian amateur came right back and said my signal was very strong and clear for an American Amateur. I told him I was an amateur aeronautical mobile station en route from Darwin to Brisbane, and wanted to see if I could make a phone patch with an American station near Los Angeles, California. He questioned my being in an aircraft, because he couldn't hear any engine noise on my transmission. I assured him I was flying at 9,000 feet, and was indeed airborne.

The Australian Amateur was not in contact with any amateur station in the U.S., but he said there was an amateur military station in the Philippines that he could usually make contact with. If I would wait he would contact the station and have it come back on my frequency. I told him I would really appreciate his help and would standby on my frequency. In less than five minutes, an amateur station operating from a military base in the Philippines, called and asked if there was anything they could do for me. I explained to him that we were en route flying from Darwin to Brisbane, Australia, and I hadn't been able to contact my wife in Los Angeles in over two months. It was about nine o'clock in the morning in Los Angeles, and I wondered if he could contact a station near Los Angeles that could make a phone patch for me to my wife. He said he would see what he could do if I would standby on the frequency.

Three or four minutes later, he said he had an amateur in Glendale, California that could patch me through and asked for my wife's phone number. She and my daughter were staying with her parents, and I gave him their Los Angeles phone number.

In just a couple of minutes, the amateur station in Glendale came back and told me he had my wife on the phone, and asked me to go ahead.

I told my wife that I was flying over Australia to Brisbane and that I had been flying almost constantly since I had left home. I explained to her that we were being patched by radio and our conversation was one way at a time, and when she finished her thought and wanted to have me answer to finish by saying the word, "Over."

It was the end of March and my wife had already filed our income taxes for 1948. I hate to admit that most of our time was talking about the taxes, and how our one-year-old daughter, Donna, was now walking and talking a blue streak. After about ten minutes, we ended the most unusual radio conversation I had ever had from an airplane, and signed off with thanks to the Glendale, U.S. Military, and Australian radio amateurs that made it all possible.

In 1949, I don't know if this was the first time an American plane flying over Australia had a crew member have a conversation with his wife at home in Los Angeles or not, but I do know it was a first time I had ever heard of it being done.

We arrived in Brisbane before noon local time to refuel for a flight across the Coral and Tasman Seas to Auckland, New Zealand. Again Vince had to wait for a gas truck to refill while we refueled at the Eagle Farm aerodrome. Elliot had woke up about four hours out of Darwin and I had got four hours of sleep before we landed in Brisbane. The flight plan to Auckland was going to take us a little over seven hours, and Captain Currie wanted 2,000 gallons of fuel for the flight. The operations personnel at Brisbane where very helpful, and when I told them we would be back on our way to Darwin and Hong Kong tomorrow. They volunteered to have a flight plan already made out for us when we returned.

We finally got airborne from Brisbane in late-afternoon Friday, March 25, 1949, as we headed out over the Coral Sea climbing to 9,000 feet on our way to Auckland.

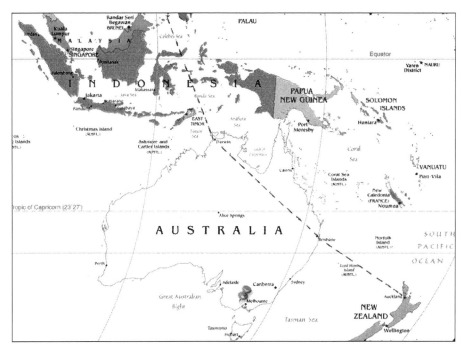

**The dashed line on the map was our route from
Hong Kong to Auckland.**

Elliot was back on the radio making position reports with Morse code to the Australian and New Zealand aircraft traffic control network every hour. There was a very nice difference on the way their system worked. When an aircraft called and sent a message to the controlling station, all the stations on the net would take radio-bearings on the aircraft's signals. After the message was completed and acknowledged for by the controlling station, the stations equipped with direction-finders on the net would report the radio-bearing of the aircraft from that station. I told Elliot to plot the bearings, and if they plotted near where the three advanced positions I had given him in the reports were, let me sleep. If not, wake me up immediately. In any case, he was to wake me up in three hours when we would be about half-way to Auckland. I was in the bunk and asleep before we reached 9,000 feet.

Elliot woke me three hours later and it was dark, and I got out my octant and went to the astrodome to take a couple of two-minute average observations for a celestial fix to check that our course and ground speed were going as planned. It took about 30 minutes to calculate and plot the two lines, but they checked within a few miles of where we planned to be at that time. Elliot's plots of the radio-bearings checked out, and I could relax for an hour or two. I could take another celestial fix when we were about an hour out of Auckland if necessary.

I gave the pilots a final heading to hold and requested they tune in Auckland's radio beacon on one of the automatic radio direction-finders.

The needle on the direction finder slowly settled down to indicate that Auckland was straight-ahead when we were about an hour out, and the radio-bearings given to Elliot after his last required position report confirmed our position. I gave the pilots an estimate of when we would be a hundred miles out of Auckland, and an ETA for Auckland.

The pilots were able to contact Auckland tower on their VHF voice set when we were about 80 miles from the airport and received clearance to start their descent. The automatic radio direction-finder was loud and clear, and its needle pointed straight ahead to the airport. My job was done, and I immediately began working to have our flight plan back to Brisbane, Australia ready when we landed.

We landed a little before daylight in Auckland, and after our passengers had deplaned, Captain Currie and I headed for the meteorology and operations office to get the weather and file our flight plan back to Brisbane. After we were finished and had gone back to the plane, the cabin, lavatories, and galley were being cleaned and replenished for our new load of passengers who were going with us to Hong Kong.

Forecast winds on our return flight across the Tasman and Coral Seas would slow us up a little and it was going to take us nearly eight hours en route to Brisbane. Captain Currie ordered 2200 gallons of gas for the flight, and I went down to tell Vince who was directing the fueling and servicing of the plane. When he was finished, our passengers were loaded and we were able to take-off from Auckland for our return to Brisbane about 10:00 a.m. local time, March 26, 1949.

Our return flight to Brisbane, Australia turned out to be a repeat image of our flight to Auckland in reverse. Both Elliot and I managed to get three or four hours sleep and we landed at Brisbane a little before 5:00 p.m. Saturday, March 26, 1949.

True to his word . . . and much to my surprise, the operations agent had a flight plan for our flight to Darwin made out and ready for us to file when we arrived. He told me of a story a reporter was writing that would be published tomorrow. It was about an unscheduled Alaska Airlines plane that had passed through Brisbane carrying a crew of a steamship that was meeting their ship in Auckland. It reported we were not on any schedule and were operating an airplane in the sky just like a tramp-steamer was operated over the oceans. Everything considered, it was not all that bad of an analogy.

Article in the Brisbane Newspaper, "Sunday Mail," on 27 March, 1949.

After checking the just over nine-hour flight plan for accuracy we filed for Darwin at 8,000 feet, with 2400 U.S. gallons of fuel. The passenger cabin was cleaned and its' supplies replenished for the daylight flight to Darwin. We were airborne before 8:00 p.m., and again I was asleep before we reached cruising altitude.

This time I got the upper bunk, and Elliot had to find a seat in the cabin. We were only two hours or so out of Darwin when I finally woke up after nearly seven hours of sleep. I noticed Bill was in the lower bunk as I crawled down from the upper, and Elliot was awake and at the radio operator's position listening to Australian stations. Captain Currie was flying the plane and making the position reports. I prepared our flight plan for our next flight to Hong Kong so when we got the winds from Meteorology, it could be quickly calculated. So far Australia and New Zealand had provided us with a very nice environment to fly in.

It was early morning when we landed at Darwin, Australia. We off-loaded our passengers so they could stretch their legs, while the cabin, galley, and toilets were cleaned and the supplies replenished.

We went to the operations and meteorology offices and completed our flight plan to Hong Kong. It was going to take us 13 hours to get there at 10,000 feet altitude, and depending when we got off, it would probably still be daylight when we arrived. Captain Currie wanted 3,200 U.S. gallons of fuel onboard for take-off, and that required there be some 330 gallons James would have to put into the plane's fuselage tank. It was good that Darwin had a long runway available for our take-off, as we were near our maximum take-off weight.

The airplane used a lot of the runway in getting airborne, but it worked as planned and we were off from Darwin for Hong Kong near 6:00 a.m., Sunday day, March 27, 1949.

We started out at 8,000 feet but climbed to 10,000 feet after an hour or so. There was no terrain as high as 10,000 feet within 100 miles either side of our route, but because of possible clouds, I would need to make sure we stayed reasonably close to our planned track until we crossed the Palawan Islands and reached the South China Sea. With normal trade-winds, no typhoons or jet streams to worry about, and a visual or celestial fix nearly every hour would guarantee that we were keeping close enough to the required track.

Our progress matched our flight plan and the weather cooperated with only lower broken strata-cumulus clouds around 1500 feet as we approached the China coast and Hong Kong. We were able to begin our descent from 10,000 feet while heading for the Wagland Island radio-beacon. A break in the clouds allowed us to descend below the base of the clouds before we reached Wagland

Island, and we could plainly see the light house on the Island and Lyman Gap in front of us. It was before 6:00 p.m. Local time, and it was clear enough for us to fly visually through the gap and land at Kai Tak. We arrived at Hong Kong just a little after 6:00 p.m., Sunday, March 27, 1949; almost exactly 84 hours since we had taken off from Hong Kong for Auckland.

**Kai Tak Airport and Sea Plane Base - Runway 13
on the right ended at the Bay's Edge.**
Photo Courtesy Wikipedia

It was remarkable that we had been able to complete approximately 61-and-a-half hours of flying in 84 hours. We averaged approximately 17-and-a-half hours a day, and had completed nearly three-quarters of a normal months flying in three-and-a-half-days. Not only was it remarkable for us, but also for Vince who was responsible for keeping the plane airworthy, and a testimony to the dependability of the DC-4 and its Pratt and Whitney engines.

We were ready for bed when we reached the Peninsula Hotel. I left a wake-up call for 10:00 a.m. so I could bathe and shave before treating myself to a lunch at Gingle's Restaurant.

When I was awakened my body really didn't want to get up. I was still very tired, but we were to leave for Shanghai early Tuesday morning and I needed to turn my sleeping hours around accordingly.

I finally managed to bathe and get dressed for lunch. When I went downstairs and checked the Peninsula's bar for any of our crew, I found Bill talking to a Pan American copilot who was also waiting in Hong Kong for his next flight. The three of us went together to Gingle's Restaurant for lunch.

The Pan American pilot told us that he was scheduled on Pan American's round-the-world- flights that were scheduled to run twice a week. Every layover was for either three or four days at each stop. He was based in San Francisco and was gone from home for 25 days every month. He had been with Pan American for six years and was still flying as a copilot. We didn't tell him of the flights we had just made, or that Alaska Airlines had barely been in existence for six years, and few of our captains had anywhere near that many years of seniority.

I did tell him of a flight I had made from Hong Kong just after the end of WW II in a Navy "Coronado" four-engine seaplane. We had taken-off from Hong Kong, to fly Admiral Elliot Buckmaster of "The Battle of Midway" fame, up the China coast a couple of hundred miles to the harbor at Swatow, China. We landed in the outer harbor at Swatow and tied up to a huge ships buoy. Soon, a sampan came out of the inner harbor around the end of the breakwater, and headed towards us. When it came alongside our plane, Admiral Buckmaster and all of the officers got into the sampan and left heading back towards the inner harbor. We thought it was strange that all of the officers had gone; always before there had been at least one officer left on board whenever our seaplane was in the water.

No sooner had the sampan disappeared around the corner of the breakwater when another smaller sampan came into view as it left the Inner harbor from the other end of the breakwater, and headed for our plane. When it came alongside we could see that beside the boat's operator, there was a U.S. Navy Chief Petty Officer and a lovely young Chinese woman in the sampan.

The Chief Petty Officer told us he had been a "coast-watcher" living on the local economy and reporting from Swatow on the traffic of Japanese shipping by radio to Naval Intelligence. Admiral Buckmaster was there to retrieve him from his mission, and he told us he was being transferred to Canton, China near Hong Kong. The young woman he had with him was a local Chinese lady that had become his fiancé, but the Navy would not allow her to travel with him. She was going to try to get to Canton to be with him on her own, but he knew she would never make it, and probably end up being killed or kidnapped along the way. He asked if we could hide her somewhere on the plane when we flew him to Hong Kong. He would come from Canton to Hong Kong as soon as he could and get her.

There were no officers present, and the senior man present was our chief petty officer Aviation Machinist-Mate, Michael "Mike" Vairo, who was our plane Captain. We all looked at him, and he nodded as he told the chief petty officer that we could put his fiancé in the nose turret where she could ride undetected, and she could stay on the plane until he came for her. She was taken aboard and placed with some water in the nose turret, and told not to touch anything and to be quiet. Somehow, I later suspected it had all been prearranged, but we all went along with it at the time.

As the Sampan left with the "coast-watcher" chief petty officer, another Sampan came alongside that was a traveling souvenir and gift shop. Because I was heading home soon, I bought a set of eight pewter mugs engraved with hand-carved dragons and etched "KUT HING," SWATOW. After nearly 70 years they still look good displayed on my kitchen cabinet.

After Admiral Buckmaster and all the Officers returned with the chief petty officer "coast-watcher," we took-off from Swatow and returned to Hong Kong Harbor.

True to his word, a couple of days later the chief petty officer from Swatow showed up in a sampan at our seaplane at anchor in the bay near the Kai Tak Airport. He and the young woman left after offering profuse thanks to everyone. I always wondered what the final outcome of their adventure together was. I know one thing; for someone who had probably never flown before, it must have been quite a thrilling ride for her in that nose turret from Swatow to Hong Kong.

After lunch and a beer with the story telling, we left Gingle's to take a walk. As we walked along Nathan Road all of sudden there was the loud roar of an aircraft jet engine. To our surprise a twin-tailed fighter plane roared by traveling up the harbor at a very high rate of speed and at a low altitude just a few hundred feet off the water. The pilot put the plane into a roll as he passed near the Star Ferry Terminal, and spent the next fifteen or twenty minutes beating up and down the harbor doing aerobatics and fly-bys at very high speed. He was definitely showing off the new British fighter called the Vampire, now flying out of the Kai Tak RAF base; probably for the benefit of any of Mao Tze-tung's agents that might be present. The jet very effectively demonstrated the superior capabilities of the Vampire over any possible World War II aircraft Mao might have available.

We returned to the Peninsula Hotel and I made sure my laundry was all taken care of, and everything would be ready for our trip to Shanghai and Israel on Tuesday morning.

I bought a Hong Kong newspaper, and spent the rest of the afternoon catching up on some of the world news. The paper reported that Peiping had already fallen to the Communist Army, and it was obvious the Chinese Civil War was getting close to Shanghai.

Bill knocked on my door about 6:00 p.m., and said he was meeting Elliot and Vince down in the bar. We chatted for a few minutes about the Vampire fighter-plane's demonstration that nearly everyone in Hong Kong must have seen and heard. Bill was as impressed by the high-quality of the pilot and plane's demonstration as I was. I grabbed my jacket and we went down to the bar to meet the guys and have a drink before dinner.

It wasn't long after dinner that the lack of sleep caught up with me, and I left the dining room to go back to my room. I wanted to wash up before going to bed, and before they turned the water off at 8:00 p.m. There was a shortage of water throughout Hong Kong and the New Territories that the British controlled, and water imported from China was sometimes not available. I not only beat the shut-off time, but was sound asleep by eight o'clock.

I slept through breakfast and it was about 10:00 a.m. when there was someone knocking on my door. I rolled out of bed and opened the door to find Captain Currie. He said we were meeting for lunch at the hotel at noon, and then we were to go down to a dock by the Star Ferry. A boat was to be there at 1:00 p.m. to take us out to a ship, where we were needed to help unload the baggage of incoming refugees. I dressed in clothes suitable for work, but not for lunch and was a little understated for the Peninsula Hotel dining room.

After lunch the four members of our flight crew left to be down by the dock at 1:00 p.m. as requested. Vince was already at Kai Tak airport working on our plane. As promised, there was a motor-launch waiting for us at the dock. We got on board and the coxswain untied the launch and took us to a ship at anchor in the harbor over towards Kai Tak airport. As we pulled alongside the ship at the rope ladder we were to climb for boarding, to our great surprise there were two Alaska Airlines' stewardesses leaning over the rail of the ship waving to us.

When we got up on deck, they explained to us that they had gone up on the ship to the north China coast, somewhere near Tanggu Bar, to pick up refugees that had left Peking when the Communists captured the city. We had been called to help with the unloading of the refugees' baggage. The refugees had been off-loaded and were in a refugee camp that had been set up onshore by the British.

The stewardesses led us down to the hold of a ship where there was a British man that looked to be in his late forties, and a couple of Chinese men, that were carrying luggage and bundles from the hold and carrying them from the hold into the gangway. The gangway led to the ladder we had descended on from the main deck. The British man was wearing short pants, and seemed to be the man in charge. He was speaking to the men in Chinese, and had not noticed that the stewardesses and our crew had arrived.

When he did see us he turned, gave us a big smile, and welcomed us in English. He explained that the Jewish refugee organization had arranged for the ship to take on Jewish refugees that were fleeing from the Communist Forces that had taken over Peking (now called Beijing) and the surrounding area. They had been brought to Hong Kong where they were being placed in a refugee camp to wait until travel could be arranged to their final destinations. The refugees themselves were being processed by the refugee organization, and we were to load their baggage onto lighters alongside the ship to transport it to the refugee camp where it would be reclaimed.

We could help if we could move the baggage out of the hold and down the corridor to the bottom of the stairway. From there, coolies would carry it up the stairs onto the deck where it would be loaded onto boats for transport to shore. To demonstrate, our British friend picked up a couple of bags and carried them out of the hold and headed down the gangway. We got the idea and each picked up what we could carry, and one by one headed down the corridor towards the bottom of the stairway.

While the bags, boxes, and suitcases varied greatly in size and weight the real problem was the hold was dank and dirty, and the air stale and humid. I'll say one thing for our British friend, though he was older than any of us, he dug right in and worked at the dirty job just as hard as any of us.

The hold was filled from top to bottom with the baggage, and every time we started at the top of a new stack we could see there were more stacks remaining behind it. I was glad I had not worn any of my good clothes, as all afternoon the sun beating down on the deck above us continuously kept increasing the temperature in the hold. After a few hours we were all sweating profusely, and our clothes became soaked with the dirt mixed with our sweat.

Our British foreman was sweating right along with us, and he got the attention of one of the Chinese crew-men and asked him in Chinese to bring water down for us to drink. Within ten minutes the water was brought to us, and we took a break every half-hour or so after that to recharge our bodies' water supply. On the plus side we probably needed exercise, and that we were definitely getting.

It was after 7:00 p.m. when we finally took out the last stack of baggage from the hold, and we were filthy, tired, and hungry. We told our British friend that we had to get back to the Peninsula Hotel as the dining room closed at 8:00 p.m. and the water would be shut-off for bathing. He said don't worry, we can come over to his place and he would take care of dinner. We looked at each other and how dirty we had become. Captain Currie said that we appreciated the offer of his hospitality, but didn't want to impose on his wife; especially considering the condition we were in after working in the hold. He insisted it was alright and not to worry that it might be any kind of an imposition. When asked where his place was, he told us it was in Victoria on the island, and added we needn't worry about the Star Ferry service being closed as he would have a launch take us back to Kowloon after dinner. Our British friend seemed genuinely sincere about his offer, and we had voluntarily worked the day for him, so we accepted.

The flight attendants joined us on deck, and we all climbed down the ladder into the waiting launch. We headed toward Hong Kong and within ten minutes pulled up alongside a dock near the downtown section of Victoria. We got out of the launch onto the dock and followed our British friend up the ramp and crossed the street towards where the Hong Kong hotel was located. To our astonishment he led us right to the entrance to one of Hong Kong's leading hotels. We looked at each other as we were hardly dressed or clean enough to go into any public place, let alone a fine hotel. Our host, dressed and in the same condition as we were, insisted it was alright and opened the front door and led us directly across the lobby and into an elevator. He spoke a few words in Chinese to the elevator operator, and he immediately took us up several floors to about the sixth floor where we all got off, and followed our host into what was a ballroom or very-large dining room.

As we got off the elevator we noticed there were people scurrying about and lights were coming on. Our host led us across the room of dining tables to a large table on the other side of the room, and motioned for us to be seated there. He spoke in Chinese to an attendant, and within a couple of minutes a waiter appeared who asked in English what we would like to drink. After several of our dehydrated crew had asked for a beer, our host spoke for three or four minutes to the waiter in Chinese. He then explained to us that he had ordered a complete Chinese dinner that we could all share. There would be many varied items from which we could choose the things we liked. Then, for the first time it became obvious to us that our British host was someone that was being given very special attention by the hotel staff.

The conversation began with our host thanking us for our help with the refugee's baggage, and for the refugee flights that we were making. We all began to relax as the tasty dishes of food began arriving from the kitchen. We were all hungry and the platters of food kept coming in a steady stream. Our conversation at the table was constantly interrupted by our enjoyment while eating the greatest Chinese dinner I believe any of us had ever had.

As we become sated with food and were enjoying an after dinner drink, our obviously well-educated host began answering our questions about Chinese customs, art, and history. He told of several volumes of writing he had completed on ancient Chinese ivory carvings. Unfortunately, the manuscripts had been destroyed during World War II, and he was in the process of recreating them. Our after dinner conversation must have continued for nearly two hours, and he gave intelligent and informed answers to almost every question we asked. We were very impressed with both his obvious knowledge and intelligence.

It was after 10:00 p.m. when we left the hotel to take the launch back to Kowloon and the Peninsula hotel. I'm not sure our host ever gave us his name, but if he did, I did not remember it until I was doing research for the writing of our experiences of flying refugees to Israel.

His name was Sir Horace Kadoorie, a member of one of the richest families in Asia, and a philanthropist and authority on ancient Chinese art carvings. He formed the committee that assisted in caring for some 20,000 refugees who arrived in Shanghai from Europe before World War II, and was instrumental in organizing the return of refugees to Israel. He proved to be a man who was not only willing to help to arrange financing for the effort, but was also willing to get down in the hold of a ship and carry luggage.

I later learned he had eventually completed a seven-volume book, "The Art of Ivory Sculpture in Cathay," and that he explained his philanthropic efforts in helping rural folk in the New Territories of Hong Kong, as enlightened self-interest. Horace Kadoorie said, "We are Capitalists and we would like to see every farmer a Capitalist, because it is only when a man has something to lose that he becomes vigilant in protection of his way of life."

Our day and evening with Sir Horace Kadoorie was one we would always remember.

Sir Horace Kadoorie (1902 – 1995)
Photo from www.rickshaw.org

Chapter Six
PEIPING THE NEW COMMUNIST CAPITAL

On March 25, 1949 Peiping became the chosen capital of Communist China, as Mao Tse-Tung and the communist governing bodies moved their headquarters from Shihkiachwang to the ancient capital of Peking.

Chairman Mao and his entourage arrived at Peiping's West Field at 4:00 p.m. local time in a transport that likely had formerly belonged to the Chinese Nationalist Government.

A China National Aviation Corporation commercial transport was hijacked in mid-air by six men while en route from Shanghai to Tsingtao on January 30, 1949. The plane was then made to fly and land at Tsinan. This may have been the plane that flew Mao to Peiping.

The Chinese Communist Army was reported making thrusts against the city of Anging on the north bank of the Yangtze River southwest of Nanking. The Nationalist Cruiser "Chungking," the former "H.M.S. Aurora," a gift from Britain to China, which had deserted to the communists in February, was sunk by Nationalist Air Force bombers. It was being reported that gold and silver bars held by the Nationalist Government were being transported to the Island of Taiwan.

Peace talks between the Communist and Nationalist Governments were scheduled to start on April 1, 1949 in Peiping (also known as Peking and Beijing).

There seemed to be more danger for us from the opposing forces in China than there was from those in Israel. We never thought that Communist agents would be able to infiltrate into Shanghai, board a plane at Lunghwa, hijack it, and force it to land at a communist controlled airport. It was becoming obvious that Shanghai would soon fall to the Communists, and the future of its stateless Jewish refugees would again come under a dark-cloud of danger and uncertainty.

As we left Hong Kong just after 6:00 a.m. local time Tuesday, March 29, 1949 for Shanghai, we could only hope that we could take all the Jewish refugees that wanted to leave China for Israel with us. We didn't know if there were any other Alaska Airlines planes that would come to Shanghai before it fell to the advancing Communist Army.

We landed at Lunghwa Airport just before 11:00 a.m. local time, and our passengers were all ready and anxious to leave. We filed our flight plan direct to Bangkok, and it was going to take us nearly 13 hours to get there. We were really loaded to the maximum for take-off, and were glad to have the benefit of a relatively cool temperature and a favorable wind.

We departed Lungwha Airport with Captain Currie making the take-off, and became airborne for our flight to Bangkok at approximately 1:00 p.m. Tuesday afternoon, March 29, 1949.

The flight to Bangkok went as planned, and our planned route from there was via Calcutta, Bombay, Aden, and Lydda. Each leg of our journey went pretty much as they had on our first trip from Shanghai to Lydda. Captain Currie chose not to go via Colombo, and thus forgo experiencing another take-off from Ratmalana for Aden with a full load. I slept thru our stay in Calcutta, and didn't even get off the plane to visit my cockroach acquaintance that lived in the water spigot there.

Unfortunately, not everything was going perfectly. Vince Weipert had reported at Bangkok that one of our electrical generators was permanently out of service. It would require a new generator be installed and we didn't have one in our spares kit. Also two of our engines had superchargers that could not be shifted from low into high-blower for high altitude flight, and one of the landing gear oleo struts was slowly leaking nitrogen and needed to be recharged often. He was keeping a list of the maintenance items that had been deferred until we could get to a maintenance base, and the list was growing. So far nothing was serious enough to be a threat to the safety of our flights, but enough to start prioritizing getting some of them fixed when possible.

We refueled and had the cabin cleaned and resupplied at the Santa Cruz Airport in Bombay, and took-off for Aden about 4:00 p.m. local time Wednesday, March 30, 1949. Again our faithful plane performed predictably, and we arrived at Khormaksar RAF Station in Aden just before 2:00 a.m. local time.

We went to the operations office and the Operations Officer had Captain Currie sign for a cablegram from Alaska Airlines in New York. We were to proceed to Lydda, Israel, leave our stewardesses there, and when legal return to Aden. We departed Khormaksar for Lydda just after 4:00 a.m. local time Thursday, March 31, 1949.

It took a little less than nine hours to fly to Lydda from Aden, and we landed at Lydda about noon local time. When we parked in front of the terminal, there was loud cheering from our Shanghai refugees in the cabin. You couldn't help but feel happy for them to finally arrive in the homeland that their Jewish faith promised them they would someday be able to return to.

After the passengers were deplaned we left for the hotel for some much needed sleep. Vince stayed at the airport to make sure the plane was fueled and ready for our departure at 12:00 a.m. It seemed our flight back to Aden was important enough that it was not required for us to stop in Asmara. We were allowed fuel for a nonstop flight, and would also be able to refuel in Aden. We could only guess we were returning to Aden to fly more stranded Yemenite refugees to Israel.

After a quick lunch I was sound asleep before 3:00 p.m., and hoped to sleep straight through to our wakeup time. I got nearly six hours sleep in a real bed in a quiet room, and slipped into the bath for a good cleansing before the crew was to meet for a quick dinner in the dining room.

We left the hotel a little after 10:00 p.m. for the airport, and there were two Israeli women that joined us on the bus. They told us they were going to Aden with us, and would be acting as translators and cabin attendants for the Yemenite refugee flight. Vince would have to dig out a couple of seats from the belly and install them in the roped-off galley area for them.

Captain Currie, Elliot and I went to the meteorology and operations offices to pick up the weather, winds, file our flight plan and read any notices to airman that were currently in effect. Bill went out to help Vince and check the plane's cockpit for departure.

After we had filed VFR nonstop to Khormaksar we walked out to the plane to get ready for departure. All was well and we took-off from Lydda a little after midnight local time Friday, April 1, 1949 for our non-stop flight to Aden. We arrived in Aden before 9:00 a.m. local time, and Base Commander Keens was there to meet us when we parked.

We told him of the two Israeli women who were to fly with us as interpreters and stewardesses. He said it had been arranged by the Israeli refugee organization, and he had been notified of their coming. Captain Currie then inquired how many refugees were remaining to be flown. He answered that at the last count there was still over a thousand, but the real problem was they were more arriving almost every day. They had officially closed the border with Yemen, but some of the Yemenite Refuge families were still making it through to Aden. He wanted to know if we could still take 150 Yemenite, and Captain Currie said, as our radioman, Elliot, was going to stay in Aden for the flights we could still take 150 refugees. Keens said they would have them here in the morning for a 6:00 a.m. departure.

We left Khormaksar aerodrome for the Crescent hotel in Aden, and it looked like we might get two good night's sleep in a row in a real bed. When we got to the hotel it seemed there weren't any rooms immediately available for us. Captain Currie had set the wakeup-time for us at 3:00 a.m. for a 6:00 a.m. departure. After we had finished lunch, Bill and I decided we would go exploring around Aden for a few hours and come back to the hotel when our rooms were to be available.

We wandered around for a couple of hours and did a little shopping for souvenirs to take home with us. When we returned to the Crescent hotel we were surprised when the hotel clerk notified us that there were no rooms available, but they had arranged to have cots placed on the hotel roof for us to sleep on. The hotel was full and there was no other alternative available. They assured us that after sunset the roof cooled-off, and a light breeze made it a very suitable place for sleeping. It was April 1st, and we couldn't help but wonder if it was not an "April Fool's Day" prank. In the end it proved to be for real, and really not that bad.

Bill and I were first to enter the dining room when it opened, and after a light dinner we went up to the roof to checkout our new sleeping quarters. After sunset, there actually was a light breeze blowing across the cots lined up in a row on the roof. The only new rule we had to watch out for was absolutely no sleep-walking would be allowed.

We later learned that the hotel often used the roof for dances and special events on weekends. When questioned about what they did when it rained? The answer was they celebrated, as rain was scarce and very much needed. Strange as it may seem, except for the inconvenience of not having private washing and bathing facilities, it worked very well and we had slept soundly for nearly eight hours when they woke us up at 3:00 a.m.

Though the dining room wasn't available for breakfast, the hotel had brought tea and finger sandwiches to us in the lobby. All-in-all, we had left many hotels having had much less sleep and food than we had before entering the crew-bus from the Crescent Hotel for Khormaksar. We could only hope our Yemenite refugee passengers had been able to have it as good.

It was quite dark once our transport left the downtown area of Aden, and no one was out and about as we made our way towards the RAF Station. The normal daytime hustle and bustle was completely missing and somehow our being there at this time of night seemed to be out of place and a bit unnatural. I remembered the people coming out of the volcanic caves they lived in when we were going to Khormaksar at dawn on one of our earlier flights.

Since then, I had learned that many of the Jewish population of Aden whose businesses and families had been attacked during the pogrom earlier were living in desperate straits. With their businesses and homes destroyed, many were now forced into living with their families in the caves that dotted the area of the extinct Al-Akhbar volcano that overlooked the city of Aden. They and their families were trapped in Aden with no way out.

Though we had given it everything we had during the last 45 days, it was pretty obvious that the enormity of worldwide refugee problem was going to require a lot more than the emergency actions that one crew and a single airplane could possibly accomplish.

Be that as it may, our immediate flight was aimed at removing from harm's way another 150 of the Yemenite refugees stranded in Aden, and taking them to Israel where they at least had the possibility of a better life for themselves and their future families.

When we pulled up at the operations office at Khormaksar, Vince was there waiting for us. He had been working on the plane since our arrival except for a few hours of sleep he had managed in the plane during the night. The plane was already fueled to 2,600 gallons, and ready to go, but he had to change some of the instruments around in the cockpit. The co-pilot's malfunctioning airspeed indicator had been removed and replaced with the airspeed indicator from the navigator's station. So now the co-pilot's airspeed was working fine, but the navigator's was not. The clock on the captain's instrument panel that had quit running was replaced with the clock also from the navigator's station, and the time needed to be set accurately.

I told Vince I would accurately set the captain's clock, and I could get by fine with the changes he had made. If I needed the airspeed I could look at the captains or co-pilots instrument panel and read it off directly. As far as the time was concerned I had the best chronometer on the plane with the Rolex strapped to my wrist. I assured Vince and Captain Currie I would monitor the clock during the flight to make sure it continued to operate correctly.

Vince also reported when he fueled the number two main fuel tank, he found the gauge in the cockpit was stuck. It read just a little under 100 gallons, and did not change as he added fuel to the tank. He had tapped the gauge, removed it and shook it, but it just stayed reading about 95 gallons regardless. Vince said he had added just over 400 gallons to the tank using the fuel trucks gauge, and the dip-stick read full at 508 gallons when he stuck the tank manually. He would like the captain or Bill to go out with him onto the left-wing and personally confirm the number two main tank was full and the tank's dip-stick reading was 508 gallons. As long as the tank had 508 gallons in it when we started the engines the number two fuel-flow-meter would help us keep track of the actual fuel remaining in the tank during the flight.

Our aircraft wasn't in perfect condition, but it was still safe to fly. We just had to keep track of the things that weren't working to perfection, and make adjustments to compensate for them. So far, all four of our very important Pratt & Whitney engines were proving their reliability, but our flight-mechanic was running out of spare-parts, and sooner or later our plane was going to need some serious attention at a maintenance base. We could only hope that the opportunity for a maintenance base came before some unsafe condition of the plane developed.

Just before 5:00 a.m. the trucks arrived with our ninth plane load of 150 Yemenite Jewish refugees to fly to Israel. The two young ladies that came to help them during the trip were also there. Though they were not trained as stewardesses, they were a great help to us as they could actually communicate and arrange the passengers in the cabin, while Vince only had to monitor that they did it correctly. Things went smoothly and we were ready to go before 6 am local time. Ralph reported the cabin was ready for take-off. So the preflight checks were finished and when fire-guard on the ramp gave them the all-clear, the pilots started the engines.

The take-off from Aden for Lydda came just before 6:00 a.m. local time, Saturday, April 2, 1949. As we lifted-off from the runway, I looked over to check that the clock on the Captain's instrument panel read the same as my Rolex wristwatch. It did, and we were on our way.

As Captain Currie was the flying-pilot he was watching the airspeed and rate of climb, as our heavy plane cleared the runway and started its initial climb. Bill on command had selected gear-up, and was watching for the landing gear lights to go out when the gear became fully retracted. My eye caught the movement of the number three engine oil pressure gauge as it dropped to zero. I called out the loss of number three engine oil pressure, and moved my eyes to watch the number three engine oil temperature gauge. The engine cylinder head and oil temperatures stayed normal and the propeller stayed steady at 2,700 rpm, indicating that the number three engine oil pressure was really still normal. Like the fuel tank gauge, it was the instrument that had failed and not the engines actual oil pressure. We had lucked out again, though the indications were bad, the airplane and its engines were really still okay.

We continued our climb and when Captain Currie called for climb power the number three engine-propeller that was partly controlled by engine oil pressure, responded normally as the RPM was reduced. When we reached 8,500 feet and leveled off for cruise, it was tested again when the propeller was reduced to 2,000 RPM for cruise power. Everything proved to be normal except for the number three engine oil pressure gauge that just sat there staring at us reading zero. It was not completely alone as the number two main fuel tank also stayed stuck at 95 gallons. My instruments at the navigation station joined the party of malfunctioning instruments, but I had my chronometer on my wrist and was completely satisfied.

Everyone but Vince had a good night's sleep before coming to the airport, so we gave him priority to sleep in the bunks. RAF Base Commander Keens had indicated he was expecting us back for another refugee flight the following morning. That indicated to us that we would probably be turning around at Lydda, and refueling there to return direct to Aden.

As we made our way up the Red Sea someone would occasionally check that everything was as it should be in the passenger cabin, and every time the report came back that the two young Israeli ladies sent to help the refugees during their first time in an airplane was really working well.

The flight proceeded as planned and the winds were proving to be quite steady and predictable. With a 12,000-pound payload of passengers and baggage, and 2,600 gallons of fuel, it would take us just about nine hours to fly from Aden to Lydda. With no passengers or baggage and 2,400 gallons of fuel, it would take us just about eight hours to fly from Lydda to Aden. That's a 17-hour roundtrip each day. If Vince needed one-and-a-half hours to refuel at each stop that would add three hours to his tasks, and he would have only four hours to check and fix things on the plane that needed attention. He would need assistance, plus an available supply of spare parts at the main stations, if the plane was going to be continually kept in good condition. So far he had been able, under our pressing flight schedule, to keep our plane safe for flight, but the little things were starting to add up.

Again, a quick call to Lydda's radio station we got a single letter response saying it was okay for us to land at Lydda with the ninth load of Yemenite refugees we had carried from Aden. It seemed that every time we landed with Yemenite refugees the welcoming crowd that gathered at the airport grew larger. We had no idea how they knew the Yemenites were coming, but secret or not, they were learning somehow. There was something very special and unordinary about the Yemenite refugees return to Palestine as their religious writings of Redemption had prophesized.

The unrehearsed joy that came from the Yemenite refugees in the cabin when we arrived in Lydda, personally affected all the members of our crew. Whatever we had done to make the flight possible was rewarded in an instant by the reactions of our passengers as their dreams were fulfilled on their arrival in Israel. We knew it was a-dream-come-true for them, but somehow it was also a reward toward our own dreams for the future.

It was just before 2:00 p.m. local time, April 2, 1949 when we came to a stop on the Lydda airport ramp, and within minutes the Yemenites were climbing down on the ladder to their new homeland, Israel. For the first time in thousands of years they were Jewish citizens in a Jewish state, and they had lived the biblical promise of Aliyah, and their arrival in the Promised Land had become a reality. I can only say there were tears in many eyes, and joy in many hearts every time we watched it happen, but the Yemenites themselves were the real heroes. Their faith and trust of the religious beliefs they had held for thousands of years was truly remarkable. In spite of everything, they had won their Redemption, and had at last returned home to their native land.

Preparations for our return to Aden had to be made, and Vince headed to the rear belly compartment where he had stored the box of spares parts. He had to dig out an oil pressure gauge from the spares he carried in the belly compartment so he could change the number three oil pressure gauge to see if it would fix the problem.

Captain Currie, Bill, and I headed for the operations office in the terminal building. At the operations office there was a message from Alaska Airlines' New York office advising Captain Currie to return to Aden for another Yemenite refugee flight, and then after getting legal rest on our return to Lydda to proceed direct to Amsterdam. Vince would be glad to hear that we were going to Amsterdam, because the KLM maintenance shops there could fix some of our aircraft's accumulating mechanical and electrical problems.

There were also some people at the Lydda Airport from an Israeli refugee organization, and Mr. Viteles who we later learned was the JDC's representative in Israel. They enquired about the usefulness of the two Israeli interpreters on the flight. Captain Currie told them he thought they had proven to be beneficial for the Yemenites and for the flight overall. Their presence seemed to reassure the Yemenites, and had relieved us of some of the worries we had about our inability in an emergency to communicate verbally with the passengers.

We then learned that the two young women translators had to sometimes use Arabic as well as Hebrew on the flight. This was because the language the Yemenites used was basically little changed from the Aramaic that was used in

Canaan when the Yemenite families had left thousands of years before. Some experts believe the Hebrew language, as used by our Yemenite refugees might be close to the language that was used by many of the authors whose writings are found in the Jewish Holy Book.

For reasons we never deciphered, but assumed were government priorities, we were informed that we could now refuel at both Lydda and Aden when we were flying Yemenite refugees, and it was not necessary for us to go to Asmara. We filed our flight plan to Aden for take-off at 4:00 p.m. local time. If I could get the flight plan for our return flight from Aden to Lydda made out, and have Captain Currie file it for us in Aden, I could sleep from the time we were over Perim Island inbound to Khormaksar until the time of our take-off with the 10th load of Yemenite refugees at 6:00 a.m. That would set a new record of over 8 hours of continuous bunk time.

Unfortunately, when we had started engines at Lydda before departure the number three engine oil pressure gauge still read zero, and Ralph didn't have a spare engine oil pressure transmitter in the spares box. It would have to wait until Amsterdam.

For our trip to Amsterdam we would also require our radio operator, Elliot Judd, to rejoin the crew for our departure from Aden. Captain Currie agreed to my sleeping after Perim Island, and decided to leave the refugee passenger account at 150 even though Elliot would also be with us.

I did wake up when the gear went down for landing, but soon after they shut the engines down at Aden about 1:00 a.m. local time, I went right back to sleep. It was after 5:00 a.m. when I woke up from the sound of people passing through "B" compartment going to and from the cockpit. I climbed out of the bunk and rubbed my eyes trying to wakeup fully. Vince came in from the cabin to get the fuel tank dip stick from the cockpit so one of the pilots could use it in the number two main tank to confirm it was filled properly. I decided I would go to the operations office and see if I could wash-up a little.

Captain Currie and Elliot were there and they confirmed after offloading our passengers and refueling in Lydda we were to get legal before continuing on to Amsterdam. We were to get legal rest in Amsterdam and then fly some passengers nonstop back to Lydda. Vince was going to write-up in the logbook all the squawks KLM maintenance could fix in Amsterdam, and hopefully our aircraft would have everything working again when we left.

I felt good after having nearly six hours of sleep and being able to wash-up a bit. We all went out to the plane and the passengers were still boarding as we entered the cockpit through the navigator's station door. Bill had already confirmed the fuel in the number two main tank with the dipstick, and was sitting in the copilot's seat working on his preflight checks. Elliot settled into the radio operator's seat in the radio position behind the Captain's seat. Captain Currie moved into the left seat, and he and Bill continued their cockpit preflight checks.

About a quarter to 6:00 a.m. local time Vince announced the cabin was secure and showed Captain Currie that the gear pins had been removed. We were ready to go with our tenth load of Yemenites to Israel. It was very near 6:00 a.m. local time, Sunday, April 3, 1949 when we became airborne from Aden for Lydda. The clock on the Captain's instrument panel was still accurate and working well.

The flights were getting to be quite routine, and we were able to accomplish our inflight tasks with little effort. Elliot was really not needed at the radio station. When the cease-fire agreements were replaced with formal peace agreements with the Arab nations, in an emergency, the pilots could contact Arab stations with their VHF radio for assistance. Regardless of our passengers, it seemed highly unlikely that in a time of peace, any nation would consider shooting down a United States registered civil transport airplane. Even now the pilots could contact the Lydda tower directly by VHF radio before starting a let-down from cruising altitude, and if necessary proceed to Nicosia, Cypress without any difficulty.

As navigator, I hate to say it, but I was really not necessary for navigating the flights between Aden and Lydda. Once the route is laid out and mapped, as it is commonly done on domestic routes, regular flight-plans could be printed for the pilots to fill in the winds aloft and use their aviator's "E6B" circular slide-rule computer, to complete the form for filing with operations. Flight plans are calculated and filed thousands of times every day by domestic airline pilots all over the world without the aid a navigator. The terrain, facilities, and normal weather conditions common to the route between Aden and Lydda, lent itself well to this option of flight planning and route flying. It was only during the active-fighting during the Arab-Israeli war that the extra precaution of having navigators and radio operators onboard would really be considered a necessity.

The delivery of our tenth group of Yemenite refugees arrived in Israel on time, near 2:00 p.m. local time, Sunday, April 3, 1949. Our passengers were as ecstatic as we were in safely having made the flight that had finally brought them home. We truly admired the Yemenite's faith and courage in daring to make the journey. They had every right to also be proud as they had just completed a journey from their previous lifestyle living in medievalism into the modern lifestyle of the 20th century. Though it had been anticipated for thousands of years, and would probably be remembered for another two millenniums, it had happened "On Eagles' Wings" in just a few hours.

April 3, 1949 turned out to be a great day for Israel aviation at Lydda Airport. Not only did our 10th flight of Yemenite refugees arrive, but on that date the first DC-4 aircraft, 4X-ACC, owned by the new Israeli airline, El Al, also arrived.

As the passengers and baggage were offloaded, our crew got ready to go to the hotel for a bath before dinner and as much sleep as we could get before our wakeup at midnight for the planned 2:00 a.m. departure to Amsterdam. Our two Alaska stewardesses were to meet us at our hotel for transportation to the airport at 12:30 a.m.

Captain Currie wanted 3000 gallons for take-off, and Vince confirmed with the gas men at Lydda that the fuel for the flight was available for us. He would come to the hotel after he had finished fueling, completed his inspections, and completed what ever repairs and maintenance he could.

Within half-an-hour after landing the rest of us were in a bus on our way to the hotel in Tel Aviv. The conversation was about our going back to Amsterdam where our aircraft could get the maintenance it deserved. We knew we were to pick up a load of passengers to fly to Lydda, but had no idea if they were refugees, a ship's crew, or a charter of paying passengers.

We were in for a surprise.

Chapter Seven
YEMENITE AIRLIFT PLANS EMERGE

It was dark when I opened my eyes at the sound of a knock on my door, and a voice announcing through the door that it was 12 o'clock midnight and time to get up. I fumbled around and finally got the light by my bed turned on. Seemed to me midnight had come awfully quick as I rolled myself out of bed and stumbled to the sink to start washing up. In a half-an-hour I was dressed and lugging my suitcase down to the hotel lobby, where the crew was gathering to pay their hotel bills and check out.

Our two stewardesses who were going with us were already there, waiting in the lobby for the bus that was to take us all to the airport.

Vince had made it to the hotel in time to have dinner with us, so I guess we had all gotten about the same amount of sleep. We loaded onto the bus, and as usual in the dark of early morning hours there was little talk and everyone was thinking their own thoughts about the day and flight ahead.

It was quiet and the airport was all but deserted when our crew bus arrived at about 1:00 a.m. in the morning. After clearing customs and immigration Captain Currie, Elliot, and I headed for the weather and operations offices, while the rest of the crew headed for the aircraft to start their pre-flight checks.

The weather, winds, and forecasts were all average and suitable for our non-stop flight to Amsterdam. When I finished calculating the flight plan it showed it was going to take us about 12 hours and 30 minutes en route, and we would be arriving at Schiphol Airport before noon local time. We filed an international instrument flight plan to Amsterdam to start at 8,000 feet altitude direct to Athens and Preveza, Greece, direct to Brandisi, Italy, then via the airways over Rome, and Munich. Except for bypassing Nicosia and going direct to Athens from Tel Aviv, it was much the same route we had followed in February when we had flown from Nicosia to Amsterdam.

We were airborne from Lydda for Amsterdam on schedule a little before 2:00 a.m. local time, Monday, April 4, 1949.

We climbed to our initial cruising altitude of 8,000 feet, and set the engines for cruise power as we headed straight to Athens, Greece. Elliot was able to get a time tick from WWV and my wristwatch was still keeping time within a second a day. When I checked the Captain's cockpit panel clock, it was already nearly a half-a-minute slow. No one was tired yet, and the bunks were open. With all the flight crew in the cockpit every seat was taken; the less than a half-moon had already set, and it was a dark-night as we winged our way across the Mediterranean towards Athens. When we were about an hour out I took a celestial fix to check that we were on course and our groundspeed was what we expected.

Vince came into the cockpit and asked if he could use my navigation table to write up all of the items on the aircraft that needed fixing while we were in Amsterdam. I gave him my chair and said I would need it back if I had to take a celestial fix, but other than that he was welcome to sit and use the navigation table for his work. I went back into the passenger cabin and took a seat while Vince was using the navigation table so as not to be in the way in the cockpit.

When I came back an hour later, Vince was still writing up what pilots and mechanics call "squawks," and are the maintenance items on the plane that need fixing. I told him I would come and get him as soon as I was finished taking the celestial fix, and he could continue his writing on the table. He picked up the ships logbook and went back to the cabin.

When I finished plotting the celestial fix on the chart, it showed us drifting a little to the left of our course, and our ground speed was a little better than expected. The wind was from the west, but was not quite as strong as had been forecast. I corrected our heading three degrees to the right, and made our estimate for Athens five minutes earlier. As soon as the pilots were holding the new heading, and Elliot had the new estimate for Athens, I went to get Vince so he could use the navigation table. He went forward to continue his writing the squawks, and I stayed in the cabin.

I went forward about two hours and forty-five minutes out of Lydda to check our progress as we passed the southern tip of the Isle of Rhodes. Our course and speed checked, and the pilots had already been able to receive the radio signals from Athens on the automatic direction-finder. I noticed Vince was still writing in the logbook, and asked him how many maintenance items had he entered. He flipped pack two full pages and counted each of the items on the pages. "Seventeen," he answered, "and I've still got at least another page to go." I smiled with a slight shake of my head, and returned to the passenger cabin.

What we didn't appreciate was that after the Arab-Israeli war cease-fire had been declared, Israel and the Arab Nations were negotiating on the terms of the Peace Agreements on the Isle of Rhodes at the time we were flying by.

About ten minutes before our estimated time to be over Athens, I went forward into the cockpit to get the exact time we passed, and issue the new compass heading for Preveza, Greece. We had burned nearly 3,000 pounds of fuel since taking off and the plane was now light enough for us to fly 2,000 feet higher. Captain Currie obtained clearance for us to climb from 8,000 feet to maintain 10,000 feet. It only took five or six minutes to level off at 10,000 feet and set the power for cruise. From Preveza we would fly direct to Brindisi, Italy, passing just to the west of Corfu and keeping well clear of Greece's highest mountains tops and the Albania's unfriendly airspace.

From Brindisi it was a routing over Rome, Florence, Verona, Bolzano, Munich, and Amsterdam. To cross the Alps flying on instruments the minimum altitude was 15,500 feet, but we would only need to be at that altitude for a little over an hour, and only then if it was nighttime or cloudy. Today it would be daytime, and weather permitting, we could visually cross through the Alps a couple thousand feet lower.

It was already daylight when we passed over Rome, and we were still five minutes ahead of flight plan. Unfortunately, the weather was forecasted to be cloudy over the Alps. The odds were we wouldn't get to see much of the mountains as we passed over them.

Before passing Verona it was obvious there would be clouds over the Alps, and we would have to climb to the minimum altitude of 15,500 feet. At least we were light with no passengers on board, and we had already burned over half of the fuel we had taken-off with. The bad part was only two of our four engines could be shifted into high blower for high altitude operations.

The pilots had received clearance to climb and maintain to 15,500, and selected the engine mixtures to auto-rich. One at a time they shifted the two engines with the operative high-blowers into high-blower, and then increased all the engines manifold pressure as close as they could to climb power. We slowly began our climb from 10,000 feet to 15,500 feet. Our rate of climb averaged a little over 300 feet-a-minute and it took us nearly 20 minutes to climb to 15,500 feet and accelerate to cruise speed. The engines were reduced to cruise power and the mixtures placed back in auto-lean. It was a good thing our aircraft was relatively light when we had to make the climb.

Vince had already reported in the log book about the two-engines that needed to be fixed so they could be shifted into high-blower. I'm not sure, but I think they were numbered 12 and 13 of his maintenance items. Hopefully, KLM maintenance in Amsterdam would be able to take care of them.

It was cloudy all the way to Innsbruck, Austria, and we weren't cleared to descend back down to fly at 10,000 feet until after passing Munich, Germany. The rest of the flight to Amsterdam was over established air routes which the pilots could easily navigate by radio, without any help from me.

We landed at Schiphol Airport just about 11:00 a.m. local time on Monday, April 4, 1949, and were directed to the same KLM maintenance hangar we had been to previously.

To our surprise, when the cabin door opened the first person to enter the plane was Ralph Cheatham. He had been in Amsterdam for nearly a week working out details with KLM for maintenance of Alaska Airlines airplanes on a steady basis.

Vince showed our log book and the items he had written up as needing repair or replacement. Ralph had been aware we were coming and had prepared KLM to put some extra men on the plane when it arrived. He would stay with the plane and Vince could go on to the hotel with us. We all wanted to get to the hotel so we could get some laundry done before we were to depart at midnight.

We cleared customs and immigration, and were waiting for transportation to take us to the hotel when the KLM lead mechanic and Ralph came to talk with Vince. After a couple minutes of conversing with Vince and the maintenance man from KLM, Ralph came over to talk with Captain Currie. It seemed when KLM had seen all the things that needed fixing on our plane, they wouldn't touch our plane unless they have three days to work on it.

An Alaska Airlines DC-4 receiving maintenance in front of hangar.
Photo: Elgen M. Long Collection

Currie and Ralph went over to the plane together and talked with the KLM mechanic's lead-man. In the meantime, the crew bus arrived, and we all loaded our suitcases and got onto the bus while we waited for Captain Currie to come back.

It seemed the big items that would take so long to fix were the two engine-superchargers that would not shift into high-blower. The engine work to fix the superchargers alone would take over two days to accomplish, but were not items that were needed to be fixed to keep the aircraft airworthy. They believed they could fix all the other items in 36 hours. The final decision was KLM maintenance could have 36 hours to work on the plane, and we would delay our departure until the maintenance was completed the following night. Whatever our load to Israel was, it would have to wait until tomorrow night before we could fly it there. There was no air service into Israel, as all scheduled airline service had stopped several months before when the Arab-Israeli war had started. If you wanted a flight from Amsterdam to Israel, it looked like we were the only game in town.

Well, we were going to have a day in Amsterdam. The talk on the way to our hotel was what we could do with the extra time. I for one, wanted to get as much sleep as possible. My immediate plan was to take a nap before dinner, then after dinner stay up for as long as I could before going back to bed. Then sleep as long as I could so as to be rested for our departure the following night. Even with the probable tail-wind we would have it would probably take us at least 12 hours to fly back to Lydda, and the busiest part for me would be towards the end from Athens while crossing the Mediterranean direct to Israel.

The best laid plans some time go awry and sometimes come out better than expected.

When I finally woke up, I had not only missed dinner, it was almost time for breakfast. I had slept for nearly 16 hours. By the time I had bathed, shaved, and dressed it was time to go down to the dining room for breakfast. Bill and Elliot were already there. As I was sitting down with them at the table, Bill asked me if I had picked up the message at the desk about our departure time. I told him no, I hadn't checked for messages and asked what the message was about? He told me that Ralph had called Captain Currie about a half-hour ago and told him that KLM would be finished with the maintenance by 8:00 p.m. and he could have the plane fueled and ready for take-off at 8:00 p.m. Check at the desk. Captain Currie left a wakeup call for the crew at 4:30 p.m., dinner at 5:30, and bus at 6:30 to Schiphol for an 8:00 p.m. take-off.

I asked them if anyone knew who we were going to be carrying, and Bill said Captain Currie had told him that when he was talking to our handling agent at Schiphol it sounded like it was some kind of government people going to Tel Aviv to meet with Israeli officials. The cablegram had mentioned that there were some VIP's in the group that wanted to get to Israel without delay. He didn't think there were very many people in the group as it was some kind of committee. Anyway, Currie told Ralph to fuel the plane to 3,000 gallons, and had notified our handling agent to have our passengers at Schiphol Airport ready for an 8:00 p.m. departure.

After breakfast I went for a walk and looked to see if there were any worthwhile souvenirs to bring home from The Netherlands. I looked over a unique pair of shoes that were really carved out of wood, but decided not to buy them. I didn't find anything else that particularly interested me, so I was back at the hotel by 2:00 p.m. My fresh laundry was all packed before the wake-up time of 4:30 p.m. came, and I went down early to the lobby to wait for dinner time. By 5:00 p.m., four of our crew were already down in the lobby, so we went early into the dining room as soon as it opened. Everybody was there by 5:30 p.m., and with the two stewardesses, the eight of us required two tables instead of the usual one.

Everyone was curious about who our passengers were, and especially who the reported VIP's might be.

It was already dark as we rode the bus out to Schiphol airport. On arrival, we all headed with our suitcases to clear immigration and customs. Once cleared, Ralph, Vince, Bill, and the stewardesses headed for the airplane, while Captain Currie, Elliot and I headed for meteorology and operations.

The weather hadn't changed much, and it was still going to be dark when we crossed the Alps over Austria and Italy. We would have some light-tailwinds instead of headwinds, and the flight time worked out to be nearly 11 hours. We filed for 9,000 feet to be our initial altitude, and would probably have to climb after Munich to have safe clearance over historic Brenner Pass and the mountains of the Alps.

When we got to the airplane Ralph had the ship's logbook, and was showing Vince and Bill the write-offs of the maintenance items that had written-up as needing repair. Everything had been cleared, except for the two engine-superchargers that were still inoperative for high-blower operation. My navigator's panel airspeed and clock had been replaced, and the planes electric-generators and instruments were all back in normal operating condition. Captain Currie reviewed the logbook, and made a careful check of the fuel gauges during his preflight. When he was finished, as soon as the passengers were on board, we were ready to go.

About 7:30 p.m. local time one of the stewardesses came into the cockpit and told Captain Currie the passengers were on board, and they had closed the entrance door and were ready for departure.

Our take-off from Schiphol airport, Amsterdam for Lydda, Israel was about 8 p.m. local time Tuesday, April 5, 1949.

After climbing to our initial altitude of 9,000 feet, we flew over the established airways to Munich, Germany. It only took us about two-and-a-half-hours to get to Munich, and we had only burned about 3,500 pounds of our fuel getting there. Our aircraft was still pretty heavy and the minimum crossing altitude at Munich to fly on towards Innsbruck, Austria was 14,000 feet, and it was required we cross Innsbruck at 15,500 feet.

In order to reach 14,000 feet before leaving Munich we had to climb while circling in a holding pattern over Munich. As heavy as our aircraft was, and having only two of our engines capable of shifting into high-blower, our rate of climb was agonizingly slow. The turns we had to make to stay in the holding pattern over Munich compounded the problem by expending energy to make turns that could have been used in making us climb faster. It took us over half-an-hour for us to just reach 14,000 feet so we could proceed towards Innsbruck. Once flying straight our rate of climb increased a little and we were able to reach the required altitude of 15,500 feet by the time we were over Innsbruck. Altogether, we had lost about forty minutes in the machinations required in reaching the minimum altitude to fly over the Alps.

After we had left Innsbruck and were over the Austrian Alps, one of the stewardesses came into the cockpit and said the wife of one of the passengers was having difficulty breathing. Our crew was all young and healthy individuals, and while we noticed the lack of oxygen in the air, it didn't particularly bother us. However, we could certainly understand how older, or people with health problems, could feel the effects of the thinner air much sooner than we would.

Captain Currie told the stewardess to tell the woman not to exert herself, and that we would soon be descending to a lower altitude.

Two or three minutes after the stewardess had returned to the cabin, a man came into the cockpit and announced that he was a Major-General and personal representative of President Truman, and demanded we descend immediately. He was standing between the two pilots, when a break in the clouds allowed him to see in the dim light outside, the white tops of mountain peaks ahead and surrounding us on all sides.

Captain Currie assured the general we would be descending very soon, as we were to pass over Verona shortly and the mountains were lower south of there. The general did not say anything, and turned around and went back to the passenger cabin. We could certainly understand his apprehension with his wife having trouble breathing.

We started our descent from 15,500 as soon as we received clearance after Verona, Italy, and everyone in the passenger cabin soon had a more normal amount of oxygen to breathe again. We were able to get back down to 9,000 feet after Bologna, and Captain Currie had Bill fly the plane while he went back to make sure the passengers were all okay.

As our plane flew down the length of the boot of Italy the pilots were able to navigate with their radio direction-finders along the established airways. When we passed Brindisi, Italy I gave the pilots a heading to fly direct to Preveza, Greece. The sun was still below the eastern horizon, but the weather was clear and there was enough morning twilight to make sure we were flying along the southwest coast of the Island of Corfu and in Greek airspace and not Albanian. It was clear and light enough to monitor our clearance as we passed the tall mountains a few miles north of our track in Greece.

After passing Athens, I gave the pilots a heading that would take us by the Island of Rhodes again, and direct to Tel Aviv's, Lydda Airport. The sun had made its appearance in the eastern sky, and with over three hours still to go we were going to arrive with our passengers in Israel at a very civil and convenient hour in mid-morning.

I don't know if any of our VIP passengers looked out to the left as we went by the Island of Rhodes, but the Israeli negotiations with the Arab Nations of their individual peace agreements were in progress there, and would be very important to the scope and timing of their mission to expedite the movement of Jewish refugees to Israel.

After passing Rhodes, I only had to occasionally check our drift and adjust the pilot's compass heading accordingly. Elliot got the one letter designator from Lydda radio that it was all clear for us to continue on to land at Lydda.

We started our letdown from 9,000 feet about 75 miles out from Lydda, and Captain Currie made an especially nice smooth landing at Lydda Airport, Israel, about 9:00 a.m. local time on Wednesday, April 6, 1949.

There must have been some advance notice given of our pending arrival as many obviously important individuals including the JDC representative in Israel, Mr. Viteles, were waiting at the terminal to greet our passengers.

Terminal Building Lydda Airport, Israel.

As we completed our paperwork and prepared the plane for servicing, Captain Currie was informed that our crew was to proceed to the same hotel that our passengers were staying at, and transportation was waiting for us as soon as we were ready. A cablegram was handed to Captain Currie that informed us we were to leave our Alaska Airlines stewardesses and Vince in Tel Aviv, and to fly to Aden after legal rest to bring more Yemenite refugees from Aden to Lydda.

Ralph was to fuel the plane to 2,600 gallons, and we would depart for Aden at 10:00 p.m. tonight.

We cleared customs and Immigrations and headed for Tel Aviv in the waiting bus. It took us nearly forty minutes to drive to the Park Hotel in Tel Aviv. We had never stayed at the Park Hotel before and it proved to be a relatively upscale place located right on the beach of the Mediterranean Coast. When we checked in, Captain Currie invited us all to his room after lunch for a quick beer and debriefing before calling it quits for the day.

After we checked into the hotel, most of us showed up in the dining room for lunch. After lunch we went to Captain Currie's room as requested. After the stewardesses and the rest of the crew excepting Ralph had arrived, Captain Currie ordered room service to bring several large bottles of Heineken's beer to the room for everyone to have during our discussion of our passengers and the flight with them from Amsterdam.

95

From what Captain Currie had learned from the passengers when he went back to the cabin to check on the woman who was having trouble breathing; and what the stewardesses had learned from our passengers en route; the two women were the wives of two very high level men heading a committee directing the American Jewish Joint Distribution Committee's efforts to return stranded Jewish refugees to Israel. The JDC was a worldwide Jewish relief organization headquartered in New York, and was very active after World War II in rescuing Jewish refugees and helping Israel to become a Jewish State.

The Chairman of the Executive Committee representing the JDC that we had flown from Amsterdam to Israel was Mr. Irving M. Engle, and his wife Katherine. Also onboard was the Chief of the supply and transport division of the International Refugee Organization, Major General Carl A. Hardigg, and his wife Mary. It was Mary that had difficulty breathing when we were flying over the Alps.

News reports estimated in 1949 that there were as many as 900,000 Jewish refugees in Asia and Africa that needed to be resettled. The JDC Executive Committee members had come to meet with Israeli government officials and study the ability of Israel to absorb 150,000 refugees over an eight-month period, and to determine the most practical way to transport those refugees to Israel from Asia and Africa.

We, as flight crew members, had little knowledge of Israel's ability to absorb that many people in so short a time, but we did have current first-hand experience in transporting Jewish refugees by aircraft over both intercontinental and relatively shorter distances.

While the Arab-Israeli war was still in force, with only a ceasefire declared with many countries and Muslims angry after the stinging defeats and humiliation the Muslim countries had suffered during the conflict, the threat of retaliatory reprisals was real. Aircraft were the transport of choice for reasons of safety and speed. Planes could move refugees over great distances in a relatively short period of time, without the geographical and geopolitical restrictions imposed by many of the overland and sea routes.

As examples, moving Jewish refugees from Aden to Israel by land would impose an unnecessary degree of possible danger to the refugees while transiting several days through hostile territories. Moving them by sea from Aden to Israel would require avoiding the Suez Canal by going south from Aden down and around Cape Hope and all of Africa to the Strait of Gibraltar and across the Mediterranean Sea to Israel; A voyage that would take weeks at an unnecessary cost of time and money. As we had already demonstrated with ten flights of Yemen Refugees from Aden to Israel, a DC-4 aircraft is capable of transporting them in nine hours to Israel, with an acceptable degree of safety, at a much lower cost of time and money.

When planning the use of aircraft for refugee flights to Israel, the DC-4 had proven to be both safer and more efficient than the C-46 on flights of over 1,000 miles, but whatever aircraft was chosen, its' cabin should be specially configured to optimize the safety and efficiency of the planned operation. That meant providing a certified seating and restraint arrangement in the cabin that would provide an even higher degree of safety for the refugees on future flights.

Our stewardesses suggested that instead of using a ladder to load and unload the passengers in Aden and Lydda that portable stair ramps be built to make it, easier, safer, and faster for the passengers and service-personnel to get on and off the plane. It would be especially beneficial for mothers carrying babies, both before and after birth, as well as for older passengers and individuals with handicaps.

As far as operations from Yemen and East African countries are concerned, all the pilots agreed that they could navigate along the coasts and up the Red Sea and Gulf of Aqaba, without a navigator. Radio operators would only be necessary over routes where High Frequency Voice or Very High Frequency voice communications were not available.

There were several other items that needed attention in order to secure both a safe and efficient operation. For each aircraft involved in the operation more than one flight crew is required to keep the aircraft flying optimally, and at each end of that operation there needs to be mechanics with available tools and parts capable of keeping the airplane in a safe and efficient condition. Last but not least, fuel should be available at each stop to refuel the plane as necessary for its next flight.

Aircraft while cruising en route have relatively little risk of major failures of equipment, but big problems can easily arise during landings and take-offs. The fewer the landings and take-offs the more dependable and efficient the aircraft becomes. Landings and take-offs mean inefficient configurations of flight, high degrees of wear and tear to engines, wheels, brakes, and flap systems. Plus, landing and handling fees that are all a nonproductive waste of money. Flying to Nicosia or Asmara and stopping just to get gas is very costly and inefficient. If at all possible, proper refueling facilities should be made available at each end of all operations.

It was at about this point when our crew discussion was interrupted by the bellhop returning with the bottles of beer Captain Currie had ordered. When the bellhop handed him the bill for the beer I heard Captain Currie gasp, "Oh my God!"

Each bottle in our new hotel cost about five times what we had paid in previous hotels in Israel. After a few moments of near apoplexy, Currie finally asked the bellhop if he could leave only half of the bottles, and return the rest to the bar. The bellhop picked back up half the bottles, and Captain Currie signed the bill for the remaining bottles. We were in a truly fine hotel with all the amenities in a war zone, and the price matched the reality of the situation.

That changed the subject to more personal topics, like when were we to meet for our flight tonight. Captain Currie said we would leave the hotel at 8:20 p.m. for our flight to Aden, and would have dinner in the dining room about 7:00 p.m. He had left a message for Ralph at the front desk. Vince and the stewardesses would not be going with us and were to stay in Tel Aviv.

I left the meeting for my room a little after 1:30 p.m. with the intent of getting some sleep before dinner. The last thing I remember thinking about before going to sleep was I'd bet that what our crew had been talking about earlier, would be similar to the conversations the JDC committee men would be having over the next few days. They would be reviewing what worked best from the flights that we and others had flown during the last few months, and then make plans accordingly for their future operations. At least they would have a base-line of time and cost to use for planning to bring further Jewish refugees home to Israel by air.

Chapter Eight
EMERGENCY YEMINITE FLIGHTS END

I managed a quick bath and shave before dressing and going to the dining room. Even though it was only a little after 7:00 p.m., Bill and Elliot were seated in the dining room and had already ordered their dinners. As I looked over the dinner menu before ordering, it became clear that beer wasn't the only thing with an elevated price at the Park Hotel. I ordered a sandwich and coffee and let it go at that.

During dinner conversation it became clear that all of us had thought about the substance of our meeting in Captain Currie's room before going to sleep. While we had all pretty much come to the same conclusion and agreed that the Jewish refugee flights we had made during the last two months were necessary and worthwhile, we couldn't help but wonder if the Civil Aviation Authority in the U. S. would see it that way, and understand our need to break nearly every rule in the book while making them. After our return to the U. S., the ship's logbook with the record of our flights would be turned in and available for scrutiny by the CAA air carrier inspectors.

At least in our minds, we all agreed that while our actions were in conflict with many regulations, they were under the circumstances necessary and prudent. We would just have to accept any consequences that might materialize in the future. There we were at dinner; after which we would be going to the airport to rescue more Jewish refugees from Yemen just as we had before. Our consciences were clear, because we firmly believed we were doing the right thing under the circumstances.

Captain Currie and Ralph came into the dining room and joined us, and everyone had something to eat before getting ready to go to Lydda Airport for our flight. At 8:00 p.m. our bus arrived at the hotel and we were all present and ready to go, so we left early for the airport.

The two Israeli women who had acted as stewardesses when we flew the Yemenite refugees up from Aden the previous Sunday were already at the airport, and had secured some snacks for us to have on the flights to Aden and back to Lydda. Ralph had already fueled the airplane so as soon as we got the weather, checked the NOTAMs (Notices to Airmen), filed our flight plan, and completed our preflight checks we were ready to take-off. It was going to take us approximately eight hours to get to Aden, and it would be nearly 6:00 a.m. local time in Aden when we arrived. We would want to refuel, load our Yemenite refugees, and take-off for Israel as soon after 6:00 a.m. as possible because of the steadily rising morning temperatures.

We were airborne from Lydda about a half-hour before 10:00 p.m. local time Wednesday, April 6, 1949, and headed towards the radio beacon at Beersheba, while climbing to our cruising altitude of 9,500 feet. None of us were tired and for once both of the bunks in B compartment were empty. It was co-pilot Bill Lester's leg (turn to fly), and he had made the take-off flying in the left seat. Captain Currie was in the right seat for take-off, but after we passed Beersheba and were on course for Eilat, he went back into the cabin.

I stayed at the navigator's station, and monitored our flight as we turned at Eilat to fly down the middle of the Gulf of Aqaba to the Red Sea. The flight was getting to be very familiar to the pilots, and they could fly the route from Eilat to the Red Sea from memory without any need for help from me. The forecast winds aloft predicted we were going to have three degrees of left drift as we flew down the middle of the Red Sea to Perim Island. I added three degrees to the charted magnetic course, checked for compass deviation, and gave the compass heading for the pilots to fly to Perim Island. They could have done the same thing themselves, as all pilots carried E6B circular slide-rules and knew how to calculate wind drift and compass headings.

Bill had tuned in the Jiddah radio-beacon and could identify it, but the pointer was swinging back and forth as the radio waves changed in night-effect (Radio signals bouncing off the ionosphere at night cause the signals to vary.) As we got closer to Jiddah the ground wave became predominate, and the needle pointed steadily to the beacon's location. Bill timed how long the pointer took to go from 45 degrees off our port-bow until it was 90 degrees abeam our port side. He then could apply the time to our groundspeed and calculate the distance we were abeam Jiddah as we flew by. If he wanted to double check that distance, he could continue timing the direction-finder needle until it pointed 45 degrees aft of our port beam. If everything was constant the time of the second check should be the same as the first.

I checked the distance we were abeam Jiddah, and it showed us about five miles closer to Jiddah than we had intended to be so I changed the compass heading by adding about two degrees to it. That should stop our drifting off more to the east, and maybe bring us back a little closer to our intended track down the center of the Red Sea.

100

We had two trips from Aden to Lydda ahead of us, so as soon as Bill had tuned in and identified the Perim Island radio-beacon I told him to wake me anytime if he wanted me, but I was going to try to get some sleep before we got to Aden. I went to B compartment and woke Captain Currie, and crawled into the bunk after Currie had got up. I rested there as we made our way flying down the Red Sea until I finally went to sleep.

I must have been asleep for about three hours before I woke up as the engine power was being reduced when we started our descent for landing at Khormaksar. Captain Currie was back in the copilot's seat and Elliot was standing between the pilots with Bill in the captain's seat making the descent and landing.

There was just enough time to make out my flight plan and get the paperwork ready for our return trip to Lydda before we would land. I knew we would be in a hurry to get everything done so we could take-off before the temperature had much of a chance to take its' inevitable morning rise.

The approach and landing at Khormaksar by Bill was executed accurately, and smoothly. We arrived about 5:00 a.m. local time, Thursday, April 7th, 1949, and were well prepared to be taking-off for Lydda with our 11th load of Yemenite refugees not too long after 6:00 a.m.

As soon as Ralph had checked that the wheels were chocked, he installed the gear-pins, and checked the power-cart, he had the fuel truck driven into position to start refueling us for our return trip to Lydda. The passengers were already there, and Captain Currie and I headed for the operations office to get the weather briefing, pick up the NOTAMs, and file our flight plan. Elliot was with us with his suitcase as he was going to get transportation to the Crescent Hotel as he was staying in Aden.

Bill started the pilot's preflight inspections and checks, and would help Ralph with his fueling if needed. The two Israeli stewardesses were arranging the Yemenite refugees in a line as they were unloaded from the trucks on the ramp, so they could control the order of their climbing up the ladder into the plane's cabin.

As hectic as it sounds, it was all getting to be quite well organized, and compared to the first trip we had made, accomplished faster, smoother, and more efficiently. Even the Khormaksar RAF Station Commander Keens was not present, and I believe it was Flight-Lieutenant Wallace that had been sent to replace the base Commander to stand-by on the ramp to observe the loading of the Jewish Yemenites.

While many of the Yemenite refugees were obviously in poor physical condition, some barely covered with clothing, and mostly barefoot, we noted they possessed a certain dignity of their actions and presence that we couldn't help but admire.

Bedraggled or not, their absolute faith that they would be taken care of and protected on their journey home to Israel, lent them an aura of spirituality that everyone, including Flt/Lt. Wallace, automatically seemed to sense.

On our return from the operations office after filing our flight plan, we asked if Mr. Keens was OK because he wasn't with us on the ramp this morning. Mr. Wallace said he was fine, but had been very busy because of many high-ranking officers visiting. Earlier Vice Marshal H. T. Lydford (Commandant General of the RAF Regiment) and Air Vice Marshal R. L. Ragg of Transport Command, had visited. Later in the month, Air Marshal Sir R. Victor Goddard, and other Air ministry and Command Staff Officers had also visited for an inspection of the Station. So the Station Commander has been very busy.

It was after 5:30 a.m. when the refugees began one, by one, climbing the ladder up into the planes cabin. It took nearly an hour before all 150 refugees had made their way up the ladder and were settled on the cabin floor for their journey to Israel.

Ralph had completed fueling the plane to 2,600, brought the engine oil tanks up to full, and was inspecting the engine nacelles, control surfaces, landing gear, wheels, and tires. The Israeli attendants had requested some more drinking water for the passengers, and Flight Lt. Wallace, had sent someone to bring more water containers out to the plane.

Captain Currie and I returned to the cockpit via the ladder at the crew door, and prepared for departure.

The sun had already been up for nearly a half-an-hour when the main cabin door was closed. Captain Currie was in the pilot's seat, and Bill was in the co-pilot's seat and they had finished their preflight checks. They were ready to start the engines. Ralph reported the fire-guard was in position, and showed the three gear-pins to the pilots before stowing them away.

It was after 6:30 a.m. when we taxied to the runway, and after doing the engine run-up were able to take-off with our 11th load of Yemenite refugees from Aden to Lydda a little before 7:00 a.m. local time, Thursday, April 7, 1949.

After the landing gear was fully retracted, Captain Currie made a climbing right turn westward out over the Gulf of Aden. He kept our path well off the Yemen coast as we climbed to 8,500 feet while making our way towards Perim Island. Bill had flown all the way from Lydda last night, and soon went back to B compartment to finally get some much needed sleep.

I checked that Elliot's radios were correctly set for any emergency communications that might be needed, and entered our take-off time into the logbook. There was nothing more for me to do until we reached Perim Island, where I would check that the pilot turned to the correct heading to keep us flying up the middle of the red Sea. After Perim Island there would not be much for me to do except take a drift-sights every hour or so to keep us close to our course.

Ralph came forward and told Captain Currie that the Israeli stewardesses would like to know if it would be alright for them to visit the cockpit sometime during the flight. Captain Currie said it would be alright, as long as they came one at a time, so that one of them would always be in the cabin with the passengers. A few minutes later Ralph came back with one of the attendants. She spoke English, and told the pilots she was amazed to see all the instruments and switches in the cockpit.

Captain Currie began to talk to her about our Yemenite passengers. She related that many of the Yemenites had told her how they had walked with their families across the mountains and desert carrying their young children, and everything they owned. They had to sleep at night in the open on the desert sand, and eat and drink what little food and water they had brought with them. Yet they had absolute faith that they would be protected during their journey to Israel, a Jewish homeland, as promised in their religious writings. On reaching Aden, in the British protectorate, their faith in the prophesized redemption was put to a test as at first they could not see how they could even survive, let alone ever reach their Promised Land.

Now they were ecstatic. They believed completely that their redemption was assured as they mounted up with wings as eagles. That is how they saw this flight. It was bringing them home as promised after thousands of years of patient waiting. It was so hard to comprehend how this could all be true, but here they were flying as an eagle to their new homeland. Both my friend and I, though just attendants, feel honored to have been even a small part of that dream.

Currie asked her what she thought would happen if the Yemenite refugees kept on coming to Aden. She believed that the Israeli government would do whatever was necessary to fully support the great Aliyah, as Jewish refugees return to their promise homeland. She believed that the success of the Yemenite's Aliyah, was an unmistakable sign that the time of Jewish Redemption had arrived.

Ralph led the first attendant back to the cabin, and a few minutes later came forward with the other attendant. She also spoke English, and like the first attendant, expressed her awe at the overwhelming complexity of instruments, switches, and levers that were in the cockpit.

She was asked what she found different than what she had expected on the Yemenite' flights. She first recounted that what she found overwhelming was the absolute faith the Jewish Yemenites had that they would be protected during their Aliyah, as promised in their Holy Book. She couldn't help but admire the Yemenites for their calm demeanor as they faced hardship and possible death with the faith that they were in the protective hands of their savior.

Then, as she looked out the cockpit windows at the Red Sea she said "I personally find the Red Sea to be much bigger than I had ever imagined. When I look at the Red Sea on a map it appears very small. Now, after flying for several hours and not once seeing either shore, I have a much greater appreciation of its size. I also have a greater appreciation for Moses being able to lead the Jewish refugees from Egypt across its northern end some 3,000 years ago."

She thanked us for the visit, and Ralph led her back to the passenger cabin.

It wasn't quite noon yet, but a sun line would give us a fairly good speed line across our course anyway. So I took out my octant and took a shot of the sun to check our ground speed and make any necessary revision to our estimate for the south tip of the Sinai Peninsula, and the entrance to the Gulf of Aqaba. The sun line confirmed our ground speed and a drift-sight confirmed our drift angle, so no changes to our compass heading or estimated times were necessary.

Captain Currie had me wake Bill as we approached the mouth of the Gulf of Aqaba.

I put my octant away in its case, and turned on the ART-13 transmitter to check with Lydda for a single letter answer to our proceeding into Lydda for a landing. There single letter answer was "P," which signaled it was okay for our continuing in to land at Lydda. On schedule, at about 1:00 p.m. local time, we turned to leave the Red Sea and fly up the Gulf of Aqaba.

Even before we reached Eilat, the pilots had already tuned in the Beersheba radio beacon so they could home in to it with the radio direction-finder from Eilat. All I had to do was log the time over Eilat, and watch the pilots follow the needle of the automatic radio direction-finder to Beersheba. Our flights from Aden to Lydda with Yemenite refugees were getting to be very routine.

We landed at Lydda with our 11th load of 150 Yemenites a little before 4:00 p.m. local time Thursday, April 7, 1949. The flights may have been getting routine to fly, but as we watched the Yemenites joyfully climb down the ladder to touch their new homeland's soil for the first time, the extra good feeling we enjoyed from actually having had a part in helping them complete their dream would never go away. Like our two Israeli stewardesses, I think we all felt a bit of pride in our small part in completing the Yemenite Refugee's ancient prophecy.

Ralph stayed to refuel the plane, and complete his maintenance work, while the rest of the crew went to the operations office. There was a message there for Captain Currie. It told us to get legal rest in Lydda, and wait for more information. I went back out to the plane to tell Ralph to come to the hotel when he was finished with his work as we were getting our legal rest, and were to wait for further information.

The speculation of why we were taking legal rest in Lydda dominated the conversation on the bus as we made our way to the usual hotel that we had normally stayed in before the Park Hotel. The guesses ranged all the way from we had flown all of the Yemenites from Aden for now and were going to fly back to Shanghai for more refugees, to we would fly to Germany and pick up a load of worn-out engines from the Berlin airlift, and fly them to the U. S. for overhaul. We had all been away from home for going on three months now, and that last guess had a certain bit of extra appeal.

It was near dinner time when we got to the hotel, and Captain Currie said he would pass along any in formation he might get at dinner time. Those that wanted dinner were going to meet in the dining room at 6:00 p.m.

I had time to take a bath, and to wash and hang-up a couple of pieces of underwear before then. If after dinner I was able to get back to bed by 7:00 p.m., I could get seven or more hours of sleep before wake-up time.

Everybody, including Ralph, was at the dinner table when I got there about ten minutes after 6:00 p.m. Captain Currie hadn't received any further messages or information yet, and Ralph said the plane was fueled to 2,600 gallons and ready to go as long as that was enough fuel for the trip.

It seemed everyone was tired and there was very little conversation during our dinner. When he had finished eating Captain Currie said he would check with the front desk to see if there were any new messages before going to bed. He came back in a few minutes, and said there was no further word, but when it came he would make sure everyone was notified in plenty of time to be ready.

Things worked out as I had expected, and I was in bed with my eyes closed for the night by 7:00 pm. It was the other end that changed while I slept. When I woke up and was able look at my watch it was 3:00 a.m. I had been asleep for 8 hours. When I got up and headed for the bathroom, I noticed a note on the floor that had been shoved under the door during the night. It said wake up was at 3:30 a.m., pickup 4:30 a.m., and takeoff for Aden at 6:00 a.m.

I washed-up, shaved, and got dressed. The underwear I had washed were dry, and I packed my suitcase and carried it to the lobby to check-out of my room before 4:30 a.m. There was some coffee, tea, and sweet rolls there for us, and I sipped on coffee as the rest of the crew came one by one to the lobby and checked out. We followed Captain Currie out to the waiting bus with our suitcases and headed for the airport with hardly a word spoken as our bus traveled down the road to the airport in the dark of night.

The two Israeli attendants flying with us were already at the airport for the flight, along with a couple of passengers from the Israeli government. Captain Currie and I went to check the weather, notices to airmen, and file the flight plan with Operations, while everyone else went directly to the airplane. Bill was in the left seat checking and setting the instruments and switches for engine start, and Captain Currie sat in the co-pilot's seat to help him finish the preflight. Ralph had temporarily installed six seats for the flight to Aden. Four of the seats were for the Israeli attendants and passengers, and two for our crew to use.

It was already light when we took-off from Lydda for Aden, about 6:00 a.m. local time, Friday, April 8, 1949. We followed our usual departure route as we climbed to 9,500 feet for our cruising altitude under visual flight rules to Aden.

The eight-hour flight went as planned and we landed at Aden near 3:00 p.m. local time Friday, April 8, 1949.

When we got to the RAF Operations Office, there was a message from the company directing us to return to Lydda the following morning and fly our 12th trip of Yemenite refugees. We were to have our entire crew onboard, get legal in Lydda, and wait for further instructions.

The flight of Yemenite refugees we were to fly to Lydda was scheduled for departure at 6:00 a.m. the following morning, and we were going to the Crescent Hotel in Aden for the night. Ralph was to remove the extra seats in the cabin, and Captain Currie told him we would take the usual fuel load of 2600 gallons, and that we would be having dinner at the hotel at 6:00 p.m.

When we got to the hotel, Elliot was there waiting for us. We had the roof again, and Elliot had given his room to Captain Currie. He would be joining the rest of us on the roof-top patio. Everyone was in good spirits and had had two good night's sleep in a row, with a third one in the offing.

Before we headed up to the roof to clean-up, Elliot came over and asked me if both Bill and I lived in California. I told him I lived in Los Angeles but didn't know where Bill was from. Elliot said he had made friends with an RAF radioman that had an amateur radio-station, and lately he was able to reach the West Coast of the United States late in the afternoon on the amateur ten-meter band. If we were interested, we could take a cab out to his radio-station at Khormaksar and see if we could get through to California for a phone patch to our families.

I told Elliot I would definitely like to go, and would check to see if Bill might also want to come. The three of us left the hotel within the hour for Khormaksar, and were at the amateur's radio-shack station before 5:00 p.m. The very obliging RAF amateur had me talking to my wife in Los Angeles within minutes. Most of the conversation was about when will I be coming home, but it was great to make contact with my family and be reassured everything was all right. Bill wasn't so lucky, there was no answer at his home phone and he was deeply disappointed. We had all had been away from home for over two months, and I believe we were starting to get homesick.

After thanking the RAF amateur for his thoughtfulness, we returned to the Crescent Hotel a few minutes late for dinner. We were the last to arrive in the dining room, as the rest of the crew had got there before 6:00 p.m.

The wake-up time for our flight in the morning would be 3:30 a.m. and we would leave the hotel about 4:30 a.m. for Khormaksar. After dinner my plan was to get to bed on the roof by 8:00 p.m. so I could get at least seven hours sleep before wake-up time. The Friday night dinner at the Crescent Hotel was especially good, and we finished before 8:00 p.m. so I was able to make it to my cot on the roof on time.

There was a light wind flowing across the roof, and sleep came easily with its cooling effect as it passed over our cots. I must have been the first one asleep, because I can't remember hearing any of our other crew-members snoring before Morpheus took over my awareness. I easily got my seven hours sleep before we were awakened at 3:30 a.m. We washed up the best we could in the roof top facilities provided, put my shaving kit bag in my suitcase and headed for the lobby.

I wasn't hungry after the big dinner we had had the night before, and the hotel coffee didn't taste all that good to me, so I ended up sipping hot tea for a morning wakeup drink. It occurred to me that if I flew long enough off British bases I might turn completely to tea and crumpets, instead of coffee and donuts in the morning.

Everyone was ready on time, and we loaded ourselves and our suitcases onto the waiting bus. It was still dark when we left the hotel for Khormaksar RAF Station, and as usual no one was particularly in a talkative mood. At the base the crew split up and headed to where their preflight work required them.

We were a little disappointed there was no later message for Captain Currie, and all we knew was we were to fly to Lydda and wait for further instructions. The weather forecast was as usual, and with the forecast headwinds it was going to take us a little over nine hours to fly from Aden to Lydda.

When we got to the airplane the Yemenite refugees were already climbing up the ladder and entering the cabin. The two Israeli attendants along with the refugee's spiritual leader were doing a good job of boarding the passengers. Ralph was inspecting the exterior of the plane, while Bill was already in the cockpit doing the preflight work. Only about half of the passengers had been boarded, and Captain Currie, Elliot, and I stayed on the ramp and watched the continuing stream of Yemenites climb the ladder up to the cabin door.

You couldn't help but be impressed by their faith and confidence that they would be protected, though they really had no idea of what was going to happen to them in the next hour, day, month, or year. They presented a beautiful example of faith and human spirit as they stoically mounted the ladder and climbed to enter the plane that was somehow to wing them as an eagle to their promised homeland in Israel.

We climbed up our crew ladder and entered into the cockpit several minutes before the passengers would all be boarded. Captain Currie climbed into the left seat, and Bill was already in the copilot's seat. Elliot sat in the radio-operator's position. Ralph was still on the ramp waiting to remove the landing-gear pins. I stood in the aisle waiting for Ralph to come up with the gear pins. A few minutes later, one of the Israeli attendants said the passengers were all on board and the cabin entrance door was closed and locked. A couple of minutes later Ralph came up, closed the cockpit door, showed the pilots the gear pins, and went into the back to double-check the main cabin entrance door.

Ralph came back into the cockpit, and reported everything was ready for departure, and the pilots got the all-clear signal from the fire-guard to start the engines. We taxied to the run-up area near the end of the runway, and completed the engine run-up while Ralph watched. All was okay, and the RAF tower cleared us for take-off.

We were airborne from Aden at approximately 6:00 a.m. local time, Saturday, April 9, 1949, with our 12th trip with Yemenite Refugees returning home to Israel after a wait of thousands of years.

The trip was uneventful and we arrived at Lydda airport shortly after 2:00 p.m. local time, Saturday, April 9, 1949. As far as we knew, by coincidence we had started and ended our Yemenite refugee flights with trips from Aden to Lydda on the Jewish Sabbath. I have no idea how anyone knew we were coming, but more people were lined up at the fences cheering our passengers as they disembarked than I had ever seen there before.

In 29 days, from March 12th to April 9th, 1949, we had completed 12 flights, with approximately 150 Yemenite Refugees on each flight. With one airplane and one crew we had flown approximately 1800 Yemenite refugees from Yemen to Israel. If there originally had been nearly 2500 Yemenite refugees stranded in Aden at the beginning of 1949, almost all of them were now in Israel. Whether by design or happenstance, we had made the last flight of Jewish Yemenites to Israel in time for them to celebrate their exodus from Yemen with the 1949 Passover Holiday in Israel.

It seemed especially appropriate for our Jewish Yemenites, as Passover was the celebration of the Jewish slaves' escape from the Egyptians when they were led by Moses across the northern end of the Red Sea nearly three thousand years before. Today, these Jewish Yemenites had just escaped from Yemen, by flying as eagles from over Perim Island the length of the Red Sea to the Sinai Peninsula and up the Gulf of Aqaba to their Promised Land of Israel.

The many coincidences over 3,000 years seemed to stretch the laws of probability, but there it was, and we could only speculate what might come next.

Captain Currie couldn't give Ralph a fuel load, because so far the only information we had received was to take legal rest and wait for further instructions. There were no squawks on the airplane that needed immediate attention so Ralph was going to have the airplane locked up, and go to the hotel with the rest of the crew. He would take care of everything when we had more information.

After we cleared customs and immigration, Captain Currie went to the operations office to see if there were any messages from the company. He was back shortly to report there were no messages yet, and he would try to get some information from our handling agent when we got to the hotel. Our crew bus headed for our regular hotel, and everyone was to meet at 5:00 p.m. in the dining room for dinner, and to get the latest information about our departure.

When 5:00 p.m. came we were all together in the hotel dining room ready to eat and hopefully find out when and where we are going to be flying to next. Captain Currie came in and immediately told us there was no definite information yet, and it seems that while further trips were very likely in the offing, the agencies that were organizing them had not made a final decision on the who, what, where or when yet.

We all agreed that our effort had been worthwhile, and we were glad we had at least been able to bring nearly all the available Yemenite refugees that had been stranded in Aden to Israel.

Elliot reported that he had heard from one of the RAF people staying at the Crescent hotel in Aden that a major Jewish holiday, Passover, would start at sundown on April 13th. On two of the six-day holiday most of the Jewish citizens in Israel would celebrated by taking a day off from work. He wondered if maybe that could somehow be holding things-up.

Captain Currie told us he would check again with our handling agent the next day, which would be Sunday, when most everyone would be back working as usual.

We were all hungry and began to order things for dinner. We had gotten up early in Aden, and most of us planned on going to bed when we were finished. The dining room would open for breakfast at 7:00 a.m., and we could get together again then.

I woke up about 4:00 a.m. Sunday morning, and it was still dark outside. I puttered around in my room getting my washed clothes together and folding them to pack in my suitcase, bathing, and shaving. It was just before 7:00 a.m. when I went to see if anyone had made it to the dining room ahead of me for breakfast.

Both Elliot and Bill were there, and I joined them at their table. Before long the rest of the crew showed up, and Captain Currie said he would contact our handling agent after breakfast to see if there was any late news.

We had all been operating on a special high for the last month, fueled by the success we were having in transporting the stranded Yemenite refugees from Aden to Israel. Though the Yemeni's were mostly of small stature, many appearing emaciated, lacking normal clothing and obviously not well, their absolute faith that they were under the full protection of their religious beliefs somehow lent a special aura of calm dignity about them that you couldn't help but admire and respect. That undefined aura turned each and every one of them into someone special that we wanted to assist in any way we could. The result was we were probably accomplishing more than we knew. I believe every one of our crew suspected we had, but we had not expressed or discussed it amongst ourselves.

It was almost 9:00 a.m. when Captain Currie went to call our handling agent to see if there were any new messages from the company. For the first time in a month our table conversation turned to what we might do if we found we were to actually have a day-off in Tel Aviv.

When Captain Currie returned he reported that we were to stand-by for further word from the company that would be coming. That meant we couldn't be away from the hotel for more than an hour or two, which limited our sightseeing and rather restricted us to local shopping. We soon found out that there was little to buy in war-time Tel Aviv that couldn't be bought much cheaper in Hong Kong, Tokyo, Amsterdam, or almost anywhere else.

For the next three days, Monday, Tuesday, and Wednesday, we repeated the daily drill, until finally after dinner on Wednesday evening, Captain Currie notified us we were all, including Vince and the stewardesses, to return home to Everett, Washington, and leave Lydda for Aden, as early as practical. He had set it up with our handling agent for us to be picked up at the hotel at 5:00 a.m. for a departure at 8:00 a.m., Thursday morning, April 14, 1949. It also happened to be the first full-day of the Passover celebration, and a Jewish national holiday, that Israel would be celebrating, while we were flying back to Aden.

At sundown on Wednesday, April 13, 1949, for the first time in thousands of years, several hundred thousand Jewish Israeli citizens were able to begin their first celebration of Passover in the newly declared State of Israel. Approximately 1,800 of them were refugees we had flown from Aden. For them, their Aliyah to Israel was no longer a biblical prophecy, it had become a reality.

That we should receive notice that our mission was completed and we were to return home on the very date that the State of Israel would begin its first celebration of Passover at sundown, was just too symbolic for us not to ponder over the coincidence.

For us gentile crew members who had helped the early Jewish Yemenite refugees complete their Aliyah to Israel under very difficult and trying conditions, the unqualified success achieved was an emotional experience like the experiences of World War II that were destined to be with us for the rest of our lives.

Because of the complete secrecy under which the planning and operations of the massive movement of the Yemenite refugee operation was conducted, it would be many years before we would become aware of the small but crucial part we had played in the early development of what was to become the largest movement of refugees by air the world had ever known.

The 12 emergency Yemenite Refugee flights we had made from Aden to Lydda, in March and April of 1949, were part of the precursor that was to bring about two months later, in June of 1949, the epic "Operation Magic Carpet."

112

Chapter Nine
WE HEAD FOR HOME

Exactly 11 months after David Ben-Gurion had declared the existence of the State of Israel on May 14, 1948, our Alaska Airlines' stewardesses, two Israeli passengers, and our whole crew departed from Israel's Lydda airport a little before 8:00 a.m. local time, Thursday, April 14, 1949 for the Khormaksar RAF Station in the British Controlled Protectorate of Aden.

Though our crew had been a part of the secret operation of "On the Eagles' Wings," flying an average of 13.9 hours a day for 39 days out of 56, we had never become aware of the overall future effect the flights were going to have on hundreds of thousands of people. The weaknesses, strengths, and capabilities of our flights had demonstrated in the most practical way, how to accomplish the proposed colossal goal of operation "On the Eagles' Wings" to fly 150,000 Jewish refugees to Israel in one year.

Two Alaska Airlines DC-4s and two Alaska Airlines C-46 aircraft had arrived in Israel in early January, 1949.

The DC-4s were estimated to have carried 550 Jewish Yemenite refugees from Aden to Israel on an estimated five separate flights before leaving Israel on February 19, 1949. One of the C-46 aircraft crash-landed at Asmara, Eritrea while attempting to fly a load of aviation gasoline to Aden. The other C-46 was estimated to have carried 130 Jewish Yemenite refugees from Aden to Israel on two separate flights before also leaving Israel in February.

Their combined effort had flown an estimated 680 Jewish Yemenite refugees from Aden to Israel, during the 45 days from January 5, to February 18, 1949. After making the five Yemenite refugee flights, the two DC-4s had to return to the United States for official testing and certification of the cabin seating modifications that had been made earlier. The DC-4 cabin seating was being modified to have at least 120 seats with passenger restraints on each plane. The one remaining C-46 was to have approximately 65 seats with passenger restraints, plus the installation of an additional fuel tank to increase the aircrafts range.

Our flights with Captain Currie had demonstrated that with the 120 modified seats, the DC-4 aircraft would still be able to fly over 1,600 miles, and by having three or four individual crews available for each aircraft they could be scheduled to make a round-trip from Aden to Lydda every day.

If you need to move 150,000 people in 12 months (365 days), you have to average 411 passengers transported each day, or 3.3 DC-4 planes loaded with 124 passengers of which at least four are children under two years of age. Because of unforeseen weather problems, aircraft maintenance, and possible crew unavailability due to accident, sickness, et cetera, it would probably be prudent if such a plan were based on five or six aircraft with four available crews for each aircraft to dependably keep flying the required number of trips.

While the math of transporting the refugees is relatively simple, the need for arrangements to provide maintenance, fuel, and facilities for the aircraft, departure point facilities for the refugees while waiting for their flights, along with Israel's ability to integrate and absorb them into its population when they arrived, is much more complicated. Such plans were probably being determined directly by the meetings of the American Joint Distribution Committee members that we had flown from Amsterdam to Lydda, and the Israeli government in Tel Aviv.

The agreement with Britain that the refugee flights were to remain secret would be further complicated as the scope of the operation widened, and the operation would eventually likely become compromised. However, as we left Lydda for Aden on April 14, 1949, as far as we knew, we had been making some necessary emergency flights to rescue refugees that had been stranded in a desperate life or death situation. We could only speculate that the Yemenite refugee flights would continue, and had no real knowledge of any Israeli or British plans for the future.

The flight to Khormaksar took us eight hours and five minutes, and we arrived in Aden about 4:10 p.m. local time, Thursday, April 14, 1949. Our flights to rescue Jewish Yemenites had come to an end.

We refueled at Khormaksar, and filed a nearly 13-hour non-stop flight plan to Ratmalana, Ceylon. We took-off from Aden about 7:00 p.m. local time, Thursday, April 14, 1949.

Everyone was anxious to get home, and we flew straight through from Ratmalana, to Hong Kong, Tokyo, Shemya, Anchorage, Vancouver, BC, and Everett, Washington without stopping for legal rest.

The flights were uneventful and we landed in Vancouver about 11:00 p.m. local time, Sunday, April 17, 1949. Needless to say, we were anxious to file our flight plan to Everett, Washington, and get back home after nearly three months of constant flying.

GENERAL DECLARATION

(Outward/~~Inward~~)

CUSTOMS, IMMIGRATION, AND PUBLIC HEALTH

Budget Bureau No. 80-R152.

Owner or operator ......ALASKA AIRLINES.............

Aircraft: .N.88786. U.S.a. .... Flight No. .SPECIAL. Date .APRIL 17, 1949.
(Registration marks and nationality)

Point of clearance .ANCHORAGE ALASKA. .... For entry at .VANCOUVER, B.C..
(Place and country) .... (Place and country)

ITINERARY OF AIRCRAFT

AIRPORT	DEPARTURE DATE	AIRPORT	DEPARTURE DATE

Number of manifests attached { Passenger .... Number of air waybills/consignment
{ Cargo .... notes attached ....

Illness (other than airsickness) that has occurred aboard this aircraft during
flight ....

Details of last disinsectization or sanitary treatment (methods, place, date, and
time) ....

Animals, birds, insects, bacterial cultures or viruses on board ....

FOR OFFICIAL USE

Time of departure ....

Time of Arrival ....

CREW MANIFEST (See notes on reverse side)

NAME IN FULL Family Name—Given Name Full Permanent Address	Age	Sex	NATIONALITY Crew Member's Certificate Number or Passport Number, Country of Issue and Date	FOR OFFICIAL USE
1 CURRIE, LARRY	33	M	123715 U.S.A. Nov. 14, 1947	
2 GLEEMER, WARREN CECIL	25	M	291842 U.S.A. Dec. 10, 1948	
3 JULL, ALBERT	25	M	2267 US.. Jan. 27, 1948	
4 LONG, ALGAR MARION	21	M	20864 U.S.A. Feb. 28, 1947	
5 CHASTAIN, RALPH WILLIAM	40	M	7620 U.S.A. June 7, 1948	
6 BRIGHTMAN, LORRAINE	23	F	7881 U.S.A. Feb 5, 1947	
7-2 DeVICHARIAN, MINNA	31	F	C 374166 HAIFA March 4, 1949	
8 MAIFELT, JAMES VINCENT	26	M	259200 U.S.A. Aug. 2, 1948	
9 Miller, ROBERT COHEN D	35	M	41 JERUSALEM Dec. 11, 1948	
10 EASTER, WILLIAM EDWARD	25	M	24295 U.S.A. Jan. 7, 1948	

PASSENGER MANIFEST

NAME IN FULL Family Name—Given Name Full Permanent Address (1)	Age (2)	Sex (3)	NATIONALITY Passport Number and Date (4)	(5)	FOR USE OF OWNER-OPERATOR
AS PER ATTACHED MANIFEST					

CARGO MANIFEST

AIR WAYBILL/ CONSIGNMENT Note number (if any)	MARKS AND NUMBERS ON PACKAGES	NUMBER OF PACKAGES AND DESCRIPTION OF CONTENTS	FROM—	TO—	CONSIGNEE	GROSS WEIGHT	FOR OFFICIAL USE

I declare and guarantee under penalties provided by law of the country in which this General Declaration is delivered that said declaration, and statements and particulars contained therein, and in the attached manifests, passenger cards, and/or air waybills/consignment notes and/or stores list are complete and contain to the best of my knowledge and belief an exact and true account of all:

Crew
Passengers } Embarked at .HOKKONG. .... Destined to .VANCOUVER B.C.. .... in the case of the
Cargo .... above aircraft
Stores } Laden on at .... Destined to ....

L.F. CURRIE
(Name of aircraft commander) .... (Signature of aircraft commander)

**A copy of the actual General Declaration
filed on landing at Vancouver, B.C.**
Elgen M Long Collection

The trip abruptly came to an end when we landed at Everett, Washington at approximately 1:40 am local time, Monday, April 18, 1949, and we parted company with each other and our dependable Alaska Airlines DC-4, N88756, "Starliner Matanuska," after having flown approximately 684 hours in 88 days. We had been through a lot together, but the best of it was we knew it had all been worthwhile.

Our four-man flight-crew, two flight-mechanics, and several stewardesses, were not to know just how worthwhile it had really been for many years to come. We had helped develop the flight patterns of operation "On the Eagles' Wings" during the early part of what was to become the greatest airlift of refugees in the history of aviation, and maybe an event that signaled a new beginning for hundreds of thousands of Jewish refugees, and perhaps in some way for all of us.

Three months before, when we had left Everett on January 20, 1949, we had no idea we were off on the adventure of a lifetime. All of us felt good and took a little pride in what we had accomplished. It left us with a good feeling and we were glad that thousands of refugee families were going to have the opportunity for a better and more satisfying life.

If we were to be admonished for our actions in flying the flights when we returned, so be it, but we would always believe we had done the right thing under the circumstances we faced.

Newspaper articles sometimes report a greater number of refugees transported by Alaska Airlines than we knew of. Because of the wartime-secrecy surrounding the early 1949 Alaska Airlines refugee flight from Aden to Israel, it is possible there were additional flights made that were never revealed.

I am sorry that neither my memory nor the documentation of our flights in 1949, provides a listing of the individual stewardesses (flight-attendants) that flew with us on the flights from Hong Kong, Shanghai, Aden, and Amsterdam.

Yes, we had experienced a lot of continuous flying with very little rest to accomplish the missions; but then I don't remember anybody ever telling us that it was going to be easy.

Chapter Ten

"ON THE EAGLES' WINGS"
ALSO CALLED
"OPERATION MAGIC CARPET"

> And say unto them, Thus saith the Lord God;
> Behold, I will take the children of Israel from among the heathen,
> whither they be gone, and will gather them on every side,
> and bring them into their own land . . .
>
> ### Ezekiel 37:21

The official title given to the operation planned to recover the Jewish Refugees from Yemen, and to fly them to the recently declared state of Israel, was "On the Eagles' Wings." The plan was developed in New York, Paris, and Tel Aviv, Israel, during the latter-part of 1948 and the first-half of 1949 by Alaska Airlines, members of the American Jewish Joint Distribution Committee (JDC), the Israeli Agencies dealing with immigration and resettlement of Jewish refugees in Israel; along with cooperation with the United States, the United Nations Refugee Relief Organization, Great Britain, and Yemen.

While Yemen, like Sudan, was not officially one of the Arab Nations at war with Israel, it was a Muslim Country. The British Protectorate of Aden was walking a fine line in representing its position as being neutral in the Arab-Israeli war. However, the English were sympathetic to the poor Jewish Yemenite refugees that found themselves in Aden basically without money, and exhausted, hungry, sick, and in danger from the hostility of the local Muslim population.

A secret, unplanned, emergency airlift was completed by Alaska Airlines in mid-April of 1949 that had flown some 2,480 Yemenite Refugees from Aden in the British Protectorate to Israel, under emergency conditions caused by the refugee's unplanned and illegitimate departure from Yemen and arrival in Aden.

When the Yemenites started arriving in Aden, the British had officially closed their border with Yemen to prevent further Jewish refugees from entering the Protectorate and reaching Aden. They then proceeded to negotiate with Imam

Ahmad of Yemen to allow Yemen's Jewish citizens to leave Yemen legally with safe passage to Aden.

The Jewish Yemenite refugee's legal departure from Yemen was to wait until Israel had completed construction of a camp with suitable facilities near Aden. The facilities were needed to furnish the arriving Yemenite refugees with protection, shelter, food, water, clothing and medical-care until they could be provided transport from Aden to Israel.

All of this was done in secrecy, so as not to compromise British relations with the other Muslim Nations in the Middle East, or to reveal actions contrary to restricting mandates on the number of refugees that were to be allowed to enter Israel. Also, there were restrictions on who would be allowed to migrate. As an example, during the Arab-Israeli War, males of military age were not to be allowed entry into Israel.

As this is being written in 2015, it has been just over 100 years since the founding of the American Jewish Joint Distribution Committee now headquartered in New York City.

At the beginning of World War I, the Jewish population in the area that now comprises Israel numbered less than sixty thousand people, and they were dependent to a large extent on money donated to them from sources located in European countries. Those lines of communication and aid were cut-off by World War I, and without outside assistance the Jewish population there was left without any way to sustain itself.

In August of 1914, the area was controlled by the Ottoman Empire, and in desperation the Jewish citizens contacted the then United States Ambassador to The Ottoman Empire, Henry Morgenthau, Sr., asking for his help in raising a needed $50,000 for their aid.

Ambassador Morgenthau contacted Jewish philanthropist Jacob Schiff in New York, and the necessary $50,000 to sustain the Jewish population was raised by three separate Jewish relief organizations. The $50,000 jointly raised by the three independent Jewish organizations was to be turned over to a newly formed committee specially organized to distribute the $50,000 to sustain the Jewish population. That new committee was the origin of the "American Jewish Joint Distribution Committee" (commonly called the "JDC") that has now been operating from New York City over the last one hundred years.

The JDC has funded and successfully managed some very complex relief operations over the years in some 85 countries on five continents. Many of these operations involve people of many nationalities, political and economic persuasions, religions, and socio-economic conditions, governed by everything from kings, dictators, potentates, presidents, prime-ministers, religious leaders, imams, to Communist committees.

The declaration of the State of Israel was backed by the JDC, and the JDC had been heavily involved in supporting its growth since Israel's inception. World War II left millions of refugees stranded all over the world, and the JDC was leading efforts to sustain those refugees until they could be relocated. Many of the Jewish refugees wanted to go to the newly declared state of Israel, and Israel had passed a law that allowed any Jewish person to immigrate to Israel and become a citizen.

Jewish religious beliefs quote from the "Jewish holy book" of the rebirth of Israel with Jews from everywhere returning to take part in the building of a great and prosperous Jewish Nation there. Jewish refugees by the hundreds of thousands wanted to travel, or as they say in Hebrew, make Aliyah to Israel to participate in the biblically prophesized "Redemption."

Thousands of the Jewish refugees had not waited for JDC to act in helping them to make the journey, and ended up stranded without help in less than friendly locations. One of these was the Yemenite Jews that had departed from Yemen illegally, and entered into the British protectorate illegally to reach the port of Aden, in late 1948 and early 1949.

A disaster was averted by the secret January-April, 1949 emergency evacuation of approximately 2,500 stranded Yemenite refugees, principally by Alaska Airlines crews and planes, from Aden to Lydda, Israel along with the close cooperation of the JDC, Israel, the British Government, and the military commanders in the Aden Protectorate.

In the course of that emergency operation, it was learned that there were tens of thousands of additional Jewish Yemenite refugees that wanted to make their way to Aden. They believed once in Aden they could find some way to get to Israel as was prophesized in their religious writings.

The JDC, Israel, the British Protectorate, and Yemen negotiated a secret arrangement wherein Yemen would allow the Jewish Refugees to leave Yemen with safe passage to the Aden Protectorate, while Israel would pay for the building of a camp near Aden to house, feed, clothe, and provide medical care for the expected future influx of as many as 2,000 Yemenite refugees a month. The JDC and Israel also promised to provide transportation for their continued journey from Aden to Israel.

The British Protectorate agreed to allow the Khormaksar RAF Air Station to be used for the flights that would be flying the Yemenite refugees to Israel. The next thing that had to be secretly arranged for by the JDC, were the hundreds of flights necessary to fly the tens of thousands of Jewish Yemenite Refugees to Israeli. It was to become a historic event in the history of the JDC, and eventually would become an epic event in the history of aviation, Yemen, Israel, and the lives of tens of thousands of Yemenite Jewish refugees. Long after the Arab-Israeli War ended, the "On the Eagles' Wings" flights from Aden to Israel would become known world-wide as "Operation Magic Carpet."

As it turned out, the original operational plans prepared had grossly underestimated the number of Yemenite refugees that would be participating. Instead of as many as two thousand refugees a month arriving in Aden as planned for, it is said at one time as many as ten thousand Yemenites found their way to Aden during just one month.

In all, from the start of "Operation Magic Carpet," in June of 1949, to its official end in September 1950, an estimated additional 47,000 Jewish Yemenite refugees would be flown from Aden to Israel. It was estimated that a very small percentage of the Jewish population would remain in Yemen after the operation was completed. The operation had forever changed the Jewish Yemenite populations of both Yemen and Israel, and the lives of tens of thousands of Jewish Yemenite families.

The flights of the operation were successfully kept secret, and no publicity was released until nearly all the flights were completed. My lack of first-hand personal knowledge of how the operation was originally organized jointly by the JDC, Israeli, British, and Yemeni interests made comprehensive and accurate research very difficult, and sometimes impossible. To the best of my knowledge, the following is approximately the way the massive operation was put together.

The President of Alaska Airlines, Mr. James A. Wooten and the JDC in New York, had made an agreement in 1948 for Alaska Airlines to make refugee flights from Shanghai, China to Japan and Tel Aviv, Israel. After having made several successful refugee flights from China to Israel, Wooten later made additional arrangements with the JDC, Israel, and the British, for Alaska Airlines to provide two Douglas DC-4 and two Curtis C-46 aircraft to operate in the Middle-East and Africa flying Jewish refugees to Lydda.

The Chairman of the Board of Alaska Airlines, Mr. Raymond W. Marshall, did not agree with the second financial arrangements that Mr. Wooten had made with the JDC, and ordered a stop to the four Alaska Airlines airplanes that were scheduled to depart to Israel. Wooten and Marshall disagreed on the cost and expenses of the proposed operation in Israel. No written record can be found of their disagreement, but it is said they finally agreed that if Wooten would deposit $50,000 in cash with Alaska Airlines to back-up his belief that the operation could be established and become profitable with that amount of money, Marshall would withdraw his objection.

Wooten is reported to have borrowed the money from Consolidated Charters, that worked with the JDC in New York, and brought the $50,000 in cash to Marshall the next day. Marshall removed his objection.

The first of the two DC-4 aircraft left New York for Lydda, Israel on New Year's Day of 1949, with Captain Robert Maguire and copilot Warren Metzger. They were followed a few days later by the second DC-4 and the two C-46 aircraft.

It is logged that five DC-4 flights were made from Aden to Lydda with an estimated 110 Yemenite refugees on each flight for an estimated 550 Yemenites total, and two C-46 flights carrying an estimated 65 passengers each for a total of 130 Yemenite refugees. This makes an estimate of 680 Yemenite refugees flown by Alaska Airlines from early-January to mid-February, 1949.

There are indications that the DC-4s may have also made flights to Syria in between the Yemenite refugee flights from Aden during that period.

One of the C-46's was lost in a crash at Asmara, Eritrea, but luckily there were no serious injuries.

After the return to the United States of the two DC-4s which had left Lydda by February 19, 1949, Captain Maguire heard on his return that investigators from the Civil Aeronautics Board (CAB), and the Department of Commerce's Civil Aeronautics Authority (CAA), were gathering information. They wanted data on the International charter flights that Alaska Airlines had made during the previous 12 months. Maguire was fully aware that the CAB and CAA were the two most powerful governmental agencies with full regulatory control over the U. S. airlines, their operations, and their futures.

Maguire contacted Alaska's President, James Wooten, and was informed by Wooten that it was true the CAB and CAA were investigating both the legitimacy of the charter operations, and the way in which they had been operated. Indeed, both the CAB and the CAA were preparing to bring actions that would levy heavy-fines for past violations, and restrictions that would curtail Alaska Airlines future charter flights and operational plans.

In 1949, the two leading United States international scheduled airlines were Pan American and TWA. After WW II, they had developed routes and flew scheduled flights to nearly every major country in the world, and they saw the Alaska Airlines charter flights as a threat to their future development. The two airlines had filed complaints with the U.S. regulatory agencies to stop the charter flights of Alaska Airlines, because they were being operated illegally over their designated routes and territories.

After an investigation, the U.S. regulatory agencies sometime in mid-1949 brought action against Alaska Airlines for regulatory and safety violations, imposed heavy fines and restricted Alaska Airlines to flights only within the Territory of Alaska. Under the new operating rules, the only charter flights Alaska Airlines would be allowed to make were six charter flights a year from The Territory of Alaska to the State of Washington.

Meanwhile, Israel was proceeding to provide for the cost of building a new camp for the Yemenite refugees in the Aden desert just to the east of the Khormaksar RAF Station, and a mile or so west of the village of Sheikh Othman. It was to have a medical station supplied with medical personnel, equipment, and medicine: a kitchen; a school; plus, makeshift temporary housing for over a thousand people. The camp was to be called "Hashed," and was to bring safety, medical care, sustenance, housing, and an introduction to a modern lifestyle that was completely foreign to the Jewish Yemenite refugees.

In New York, James Wooten met with Raymond Marshall, and argued that Alaska Airlines was flying humanitarian flights rescuing Jewish refugees from persecution, in direct cooperation with the American Jewish Joint Distribution Committee. The flights were in compliance and cooperation with Israel, the United Nation Refugee Relief Organization, U.S. State Department policy, and the sympathetic approval of the recently reelected U. S. President Harry Truman. Wooten believed that Alaska Airlines was doing the right thing, and should continue its plan to contract with the JDC to engage in more refugee flights.

At the same time, Wooten was to encourage, through the JDC, the Israeli government, UNRRO, the White House, and the U. S. State Department, to bring pressure on the CAB and CAA to remove the proposed ban on Alaska Airlines making international charter flights on humanitarian grounds.

In New York during April of 1949, James Wooten tendered his resignation as President of Alaska Airlines to Alaska's Chairman of the Board, Raymond Marshall. The available records indicate Wooten's resignation from Alaska Airlines did not become official until October 14, of 1949.

In response to the regulatory actions against Alaska Airlines, James Wooten began planning the formation of a new airline to fly Jewish refugees to Israel that would be equipped with Douglas DC-4 and Curtis C-46 aircraft. The cabins would be specially designed and equipped to transport refugees from Yemen, and other Muslim nations in Asia and Africa. The airline would be called Near

East Air Transport (NEAT), and would technically be a new U.S. non-scheduled airline based in New York.

Wooten announced that the Flight Manager of Operations for Near East Air Transport would be Captain Robert F. Maguire Jr., and the Chief pilot would be Captain Henry Mullineaux.

Wooten was not one to let grass grow under his feet, or let an opportunity pass-by without timely action. Between April and October of 1949, he had put together a new U. S. airline, and negotiated a deal with the JDC, the Israeli Government, various refugee organizations, and the recently formed Israeli Airline, El Al, to fly Jewish refugees from Asia and Africa to Israel with aircraft and crews leased from various other U.S. Airlines that had underutilized equipment and crews available.

The overall plan could provide Near East Air Transport with as many DC-4 aircraft and crews, as required to operate JDC's operation "On the Eagles' Wings." He would pay the airlines from which he had leased the DC-4 equipment $1.25 for each mile of a trip that their aircraft and crews completed. Under relatively similar terms, for each mile that a leased C-46 and crew completed, the lessor would also receive an appropriate amount. Near East Air Transport would only have to provide the management, operations, fuel, and maintenance staff as needed.

During the negotiations, the Israeli Airline, El Al, obtained a 20 percent interest in the Near East Air Transport (NEAT) operation, and would gain operational experience that would prove to be very valuable in the development of El Al's future airline operations. The 20 percent of NEAT's profits would also be very useful during the cash-strapped new Israeli airline's start-up period.

In May of 1949, Yemen's Imam signed a decree allowing the Jews of Yemen to leave. The announcement spread rapidly throughout the country and the Jewish population began to react almost immediately.

By June of 1949, the still unfinished camp called Hashed in the Aden Protectorate was already over-crowded with a thousand Jewish Yemenites waiting for transportation to Israel. Unfortunately, there were more Jewish Yemenite refugees arriving daily.

Wooten had NEAT lease two of Alaska Airlines DC-4s with modified seating and crews, and the Flying Tiger Line was to lease to NEAT up to five more seating modified DC-4s with crews when required. NEAT would soon have available as many as seven DC-4s along with crews ready for transporting Jewish Yemenite refugees from Khormaksar RAF Station in Aden to Lydda, Israel. All seven of the DC-4s would have their seating modified so they could carry approximately 120 refugees, and on the C-46s, approximately 70 refugees on each trip.

James "Jimmy" Wooten the President of NEAT, Robert "Bob" Maguire, the Director of Operations, and Henry "Hank" Mullineaux, the Chief Pilot, had been very busy producing maps and operating manuals for the pilots of the airlines who were on lease to NEAT to use during their flights between Aden, Lydda, Nicosia, and Asmara. They were made up to be like the charts and manuals that they had used in their previous experiences around the world, but were not available for the routes they were to fly with the refugees flying to Israel. Fortunately, all the leased planes and crews were experienced in flying internationally, and all were current and qualified by their own airline. Chief Pilot Hank Mullineaux, only had to brief the crews, and if they seemed to be having any difficulty, to fly with them on a trip to make sure they were conforming to the routes as directed.

While the Arab- Israeli War had ended on March 10, 1949, Israel's War of Independence had not ended, and the Jewish Yemenite refugee flights still needed to be carefully flown by the safest routes possible to protect their passengers.

James Wooten was also working on the fuel and maintenance issues. In conferences with the JDC and Israeli interests, he had convinced them that they were in a better position to handle the fuel issue than he was. To make it worth their while, NEAT would purchase all their fuel, in Lydda and Aden, from any JDC or Israeli fuel company at the standard retail price, and deduct its cost from the payment of the refugee's fares.

As for heavy aircraft maintenance that could not be handled by the mechanics he would station in Lydda and Aden, Wooten had sent Ralph Cheatham to Amsterdam to make arrangements with KLM to do any required heavy maintenance on NEAT's aircraft, and to overhaul defective parts from maintenance so they could be reused when necessary on NEAT's aircraft. At least to begin with, the planes were going to have to fly to Nicosia and Asmara on their trips until fuel could be arranged for them in Lydda, Israel and at the Khormaksar RAF Station in Aden.

The NEAT flights from Aden to Lydda were to begin in June of 1949, and it was estimated that operation "On the Eagles' Wings" might eventually have as many as 20 to 30 thousand Yemenite refugees to be evacuated.

By July of 1949, James Wooten had completed the arrangements for NEAT to lease seven DC-4 aircraft modified to carry up to 120 passengers with the name "Near East Air Transport" painted on their sides, along with crews available for each plane. The seven leased aircraft and crews would be able to fly as many as 840 Yemenite refugees each day from Aden to Lydda for the JDC and Israel for operation "On the Eagles' Wings."

This would provide Israel and the JDC with a phenomenally low transportation cost of approximately six cents per refugee mile to fly the Yemenite refugees on DC-4's from Aden to Lydda, Israel. As Mr. Wooten said, he was never one to pass-up making a quick buck. Not only were the Israeli refugee organizations and the JDC getting a great price, but El Al, NEAT, and Mr. Wooten would also benefit financially. When fuel became available in both Lydda and Aden, NEAT's costs for the Aden to Lydda Yemenite refugee flights would drop by at least 15 percent, and NEAT's profits would soar by more than a third.

Regardless of how you looked at it, Jimmy Wooten was a remarkable innovator, negotiator, and executive that could get things done regardless of the handicaps that faced him. It is unlikely that operation "On the Eagles' Wings," would have got off to as good a start as it did if it hadn't been for his talents and drive.

Actually, as far as the starting of an airline is concerned, it is hard to imagine how NEAT's having the airplanes and trained crews supplied on a lease arrangement without any investment of money by NEAT was worth its weight in gold. Just how much of that had to do with El Al's 20 percent interest in NEAT is unknown, but it was an arrangement that was to later benefit almost everyone who participated in the Yemenite refugee airlift.

Unfortunately, the best laid plans can sometimes go amiss. The DC-4 aircraft seating plans were approved by the CAA, but before entering service in Israel at the beginning of 1949, they had not demonstrated the effectiveness or abilities of the passenger restraint system, or the ability of 120 passengers to be able to evacuate the aircraft in compliance with the regulatory requirements. In January of 1949, the Alaska Airlines planes had left for Israel as soon as the seating was installed, and before the regulatory agencies had inspected and tested the installation. It is understandable that the pressure to get the Yemenite refugee flights operating was having an effect on everyone to make it happen without delay.

However, the U. S. Civil Aeronautics Authority did not see it that way, and they had Alaska Airlines bring the aircraft back to the U.S. to complete the certification process. After the certification was finally completed, the U.S. Civil Aeronautics Board's and U.S. Civil Aeronautics Authority's regulatory actions further delayed the Alaska Airlines aircraft from being cleared for departure from the U.S.

None of the Alaska Airlines modified DC-4's had reached Aden by early June of 1949 when operation "On the Eagles Wings" was to start. In mid-June, the British alerted the Israelis that they might have as many as twenty thousand Yemenites arrive at Hashed before the end of August.

Finally, on June 28, 1949 the first Alaska Airlines DC-4 arrived in Aden, and carried 108 Yemenite refugees to Lydda. On June 30, 1949 a second flight from Aden to Lydda was completed. So far, all this had occurred before the camp at Hashed was even officially opened. Four days later, the Hashed camp was finally opened on July 4, 1949, though construction to expand the facilities was to continue for several more months.

The next flight from Aden was by an Alaska Airlines DC-4 on July 7, 1949, when approximately 100 Yemenite refugees were flown to from Aden to Lydda. It was to be the last flight that an Alaska Airlines DC-4 would make from Aden, as the DC-4 had to return to the United States to be repainted and officially transferred under lease to Near East Air Transport.

During the rest of July, an Alaska Airlines Curtis C-46 was the only plane available to fly the Yemenite refugees from Aden to Lydda. It managed about 7 flights averaging about 61 refugees on each flight, before it was rendered inoperable by the failure of one of its engines.

Between June 1, and July 31, 1949 approximately 733 Yemenite refugees had been flown from Aden to Lydda while over twelve hundred new Yemenites had arrived at camp Hashed in Aden. It was reported by the British that they were holding another thousand Jewish Yemenites at several border crossings while work at the Hashed camp continued to increase its available facilities.

When the Alaska Airlines DC-4 that had returned to the United States for repainting and leasing to Near East Air Transport tried to leave New York for Israel, it was denied permission to depart. The U. S. State Department and the U. S. Department of Commerce were in conference to decide if it was legal for the newly formed NEAT airline to depart the United States with a leased Alaska Airlines DC-4. Nothing bureaucratic happens very fast, but in the end, Wooten won and the leased Alaska Airlines DC-4 was allowed to depart from the United States on August 8, 1949 as a flight of the newly formed U. S. Airline, Near East Air Transport.

The day before, on August 7, 1949, Alaska Airlines had notified the JDC in New York that the refugee airlift contract had been officially turned over to Near East Air Transport.

On August 11, 1949, Captain "Bob" Maguire arrived at Lydda with the first DC-4 Near East Air Transport had leased from Alaska Airlines, along with a replacement engine for the C-46. After taking a rest and off-loading the C-46 engine, he left at midnight for Aden to make the first DC-4 trip of Wooten's new airline. The Near East Air Transport departed from Aden to Lydda carrying Jewish Yemenite refugees on operation "On the Eagles' Wings." This operation that was to become known publicly as "The Magic Carpet," was finally underway.

A second Near East Air Transport DC-4 leased from Alaska Airlines arrived before the end of August, but by then it was obvious that NEAT needed to lease more aircraft to move the Jewish Yemenite refugees expeditiously. There was already a large backlog of refugees at Camp Hashed, and everyday a greater number of refugees were arriving at the camp than NEAT was able to fly out.

When the information that it was necessary for NEAT to increase its DC-4 fleet to meet the demand for more refugee flights from Aden reached James Wooten in New York, he immediately finalized the arrangements with Robert W. Prescott, President of the Flying Tiger Line, to supply five DC-4s with crews. The DC-4 cabins had been configured for the Jewish Yemenite refugee operation, and would have Near East Air Transport painted in large letters on each side of the upper fuselage with any Flying Tiger Line identity markings painted over.

Five more leased DC-4's with crews from the Flying Tiger Line, would bring Near East Air Transport's DC-4 fleet up to seven aircraft, which would be capable of flying as many as seven trips, carrying 840 passengers, every day. This provided Wooten and NEAT with the capacity to not only catch up with the refugee backload in Aden, but to also take on other needed refugee operations when required.

The multi-nationally arranged plan agreed upon by the parties involved envisioned an orderly and controlled exodus of the Yemenite Jews from Yemen with a controlled steady flow of them into the Hashed camp in Aden. Once there it was envisioned the refugees would be processed and prepared for their flight to Lydda, and Israel would be prepared to receive them in an orderly manner.

It is also reported that a British airline had made flights from Aden to Lydda with an Avro Tudor aircraft, but withdrew because of the extremely harsh environmental conditions the aircraft encountered when flying between Aden and Lydda.

Though the British had alerted them that there might be five to ten thousand Yemenite refugees arriving by the end of August, 1949; neither the Israelis nor the JDC had anticipated the deluge of Jewish Yemenite refugees that were soon to inundate Hashed, as well as Near East Air Transport, and the flights of "The Magic Carpet" from Aden to Lydda.

NEAT was able to mobilize the additional DC-4 aircraft and crews from The Flying Tiger Line, Alaska Airlines, Seaboard, and others. Before the end on 1949, the timely movement of Jewish Yemenite refugees from Aden to Lydda was beginning to come under control. During 1950, as the required number of flights of Yemenite refugees diminished, the leased planes could be returned to the lessee, or placed for use on other refugee charter operations.

Later, on August 26, 1950, El Al even painted one of its' DC-4s, 4X-AND, as a Near East Air Transport plane, and flew Yemenite refugees from Aden to Lydda. El Al, was planning to expand its flight operations into Europe and across the Atlantic to New York. The 20% interest El Al had in NEAT was benefitting both airlines in many ways, and often Near East Air Transport was known to use El Al crew members on their refugee flights.

Before "Operation Magic Carpet" was officially ended in October of 1950, it is estimated that nearly 50,000 Jewish Yemenite refugees had successfully been flown from Aden to Lydda without a single loss of life that was attributed to the Eagles that flew them.

There has been criticism of the planning and management of the flow of the Jewish Yemenite refugees into the Aden Protectorate, as well as controversy over the facilities and care the refugees received at the Hashed camp in the beginning. Criticism has also been made of the reception and facilities afforded the refugees after they arrived in Israel, but I cannot remember hearing of a single complaint or disparaging remark from any of the more than 2,000 refugees that we flew.

When I interviewed Captain Al Silver of the Flying Tiger Line, who flew the Yemenite refugees during 1950, he remarked how deeply he had been affected by the near 600 graves he saw of the Yemenite refugees that had died and were buried at a cemetery near Hashed.

Though no one had died or any children been born on any of the flights I was on, I am sure that when dealing with some 50,000 people both natural deaths and births would occur. While both of the events may have happened, hopefully it would actually be more babies born while being transported than refugees dying of natural causes while making their Aliyah. I am grateful that none happened because of the operation of our flights.

After flying more than 400 flights, the secret operation was ended, but it would still be several months before the flights would be revealed to the public. Besides being labeled "Operation Magic Carpet," at one point the Yemeni flights had also been referred to as "Operation Messiah's Coming."

By the early experimenting and adjusting of the best and most practical ways to fly the Jewish Yemenite refugees on their Aliyah to Israel, the Joint

Distribution Committee, Israel, Alaska Airlines, El Al, James Wooten, Captain Robert Maguire, Captain Hank Mullineaux, Captain John Thompson, Captain Sam Lewis, Captain Sam Silver, Captain Warren Metzger, and last but not least, Captain Larry Currie and his ironmen crew, all deserve special credit above and beyond all expectations for the selfless dedication of their skills in making "Operation Magic Carpet" one of the most successful civil aviation refugee evacuation feats of all time, and truly an epic event in aviation history. But, while their actions were indeed exemplary and helped make it possible, they are not the ones deserving the highest praise.

The credit for the Aliyah of the Yemenites to Israel truly belongs to the Jewish Yemenite refugees themselves. They were the ones who gave up the security of their homes and most of their worldly goods, many walking barefoot across hundreds of miles of mountains and deserts carrying their young, their religious writings, and their few worldly possessions to face an unknown future. They were the ones with the fortitude and faith to trust in the words written in the "Jewish holy book" they carried, that they would somehow be able to complete their journey safely, and have a better life when they reached the promised-land.

A Yemenite family walking through the desert to a reception camp set up by the JDC near Aden.
Photo by Kluger Zoltan; Courtesy of Israeli National Photo Archive

Chapter Eleven
THE PROMISED LAND

> In the same day the Lord made a covenant with Abram,
> saying, Unto thy seed have I given this land,
> from the river of Egypt unto the great river,
> the river Euphrates
>
> **Genesis 15:18**

"Operation Magic Carpet" was a great model for moving refugees and large numbers of people safely and economically when required. Israel, the JDC, El Al, and NEAT were to put it to good use on many other refugee operations.

As mentioned earlier, "Operation Ezra" brought Jewish refugees home to Israel from Syria. Ezra was also referred to as "Operation Ali Baba" and in the end was an even larger operation than the flights from Yemen. It was started in May of 1950, before "Operation Magic Carpet" was completed. El Al played a large role in the operation, and often supplied flight-crew members and cabin attendants for the flights.

Some of the airlines that supplied aircraft and crews to Near East Air Transport for "Operation Magic Carpet" were Alaska Airlines, El Al, The Flying Tiger Line, Seaboard, and Transocean Airline. The British operated the number two prototype of the Avro Tudor II aircraft G-AGRY to fly Jewish Yemenites Refugees from Aden in tropical trials of the aircraft's capabilities.

From late 1950 until the end of 1952, a little known participant in the flights of "The Magic Carpet" and "Operation Ali Baba" was the Cuban airline Intercontinental Aerea de Cuba S.A. The agreement with Iran, Iraq, and India specified there would be no direct flights between the participating countries and Israel. That required all flights to make a stop in Nicosia, Cypress before landing in Lydda. It was arranged by El Al that Intercontinental Aerea de Cuba S.A. would fly their C-46 aircraft with Cuban pilots on "Operation Ali Baba," out of a local office they established in Nicosia, Cypress. Flying their C-46s to Baghdad and Basra in Iraq, Teheran in Iran, and Bombay in India, during the two years of operating on "Operation Ali Baba," the Cuban airline was reported to have flown more than 110,000 refugees to Israel.

Many other refugee rescue missions following the "Magic Carpet" were flown using the proven model of operation. Over the next few years many refugee rescue operations were successful in providing Aliyah to 300,000 Jewish refugees from North Africa to Israel. Many of those operations were given names like Moses, Joshua, Yachin, and their successes were widely reported.

But to me, one of the most outstanding and interesting operations was the covert Israeli military operation to recover Ethiopian Jews from Ethiopia, and bring them to Israel. An all Israeli fleet of 35 aircraft including Israeli Military Lockheed C-130s and El Al Boeing 747s were included. The secret operation was called "Operation Solomon," and required the operation to secretly remove over 14,000 Ethiopian Jews in 36 hours. When push came to shove, the emergency techniques they used to make the operation possible, I found very interesting and familiar.

To be able to remove the threatened Jewish population from Ethiopia to Israel within the 36-hour time frame provided by the covert plan of "Operation Solomon," it was required for them to strip all the seats from planes so they could carry more passengers. Probably the greatest number of people ever on an airplane in flight occurred during that operation.

On Friday, May 24, 1991 an El Al Boeing 747 took off from Ethiopia and landed five-and-a-half hours later in Israel with 1,122 passengers on board. I'll repeat that in case you think it might be a miss-print. An El Al Boeing 747 flew from Ethiopia to Israel with 1,122 passengers on board during "Operation Solomon."

A Boeing 747 can normally be configured to have a seating arrangement that will accommodate about 450 passengers, so the EL AL plane was carrying nearly two-and-a-half times its' normal maximum number of passengers. 42 years earlier our Alaska Airlines Douglas DC-4 could normally carry a maximum of about 50 passengers, and we carried 150, or three times its' normal maximum capacity.

My hats-off to "Operation Solomon," the Israeli Military, and El Al for removing from harms-way in 36 hours 14,325 Jewish Ethiopian refugees and bringing them safely home to Israel.

Just an observation of coincidence with our March 12, 1949 first flight of Yemenites, "Operation Solomon" also operated on Saturday the Sabbath day for Jews in 1991. I was to find out later, that Jewish law actually encourages violation of the Sabbath if it is to save lives

The emergency decision we made on the ramp at Khormaksar RAF Station in 1949, seems to be valid to this day when emergency life and death situations are confronted. Note the photo of the interior of this Tennessee National Guard C-17 aircraft evacuating people in jeopardy from Tacloban to Manila in the Philippines, after Super-Typhoon Haiyan had devastated the area on November 8, 2013 local Philippines time.

A lack of crew-rest periods, or normal seating and seat-belts, are ignored when you are confronted with a life or death situation if the refugees are left behind. The following photograph may give the reader some idea of what the inside of the El Al Boeing 747 might have looked like when flying with 1,122 passengers in 1992, or that of our Alaska Airlines Douglas DC-4 with 150 passengers onboard in 1949. Only the early emergency flights evacuating the Jewish Yemenites from Aden were flown this way. The flights of "Operation Magic Carpet" by NEAT were flown with approved seating and passenger restraint.

2013 Military C-17 Aircraft evacuating Tacloban refugees from Typhoon Haiyan.
U.S. Air Force, Tennessee National Guard Photo.

When Israel became a state in 1948, its population was about 806,000. By the end of 1949, over 340,000 immigrants and refugees had increased its population by more than 42 percent to 1,146,000. From 1948, to when this is being written in 2015, Israel's population has increased seven-fold to approximately 8,400,000.

It was very difficult for Israel in 1950, when the refugees began continuously arriving in ever increasing numbers, to supply them with a place to live and to integrate them into meaningful and productive jobs with Israel's new and financially pressed war-time economy.

In 1949 nearly 250,000 refugees arrived in Israel, and the only place they had available to put them were in tent camps and unused military barracks. The cost to transport, house, feed, and care for the immigrating refugee was overwhelming to the Israeli government, and came close to causing it to have a financial collapse.

When the Yemenite refugees arrived from Aden on our flights, they were offloaded from our plane onto the ramp at Lydda, and transferred by trucks to temporary camps where they had put up tents to house the refugees until suitable transit camps could be built.

The transition for all of the immigrants was difficult, but especially so for the Yemenites. The Yemenites could handle the lack of ordinary facilities that were not provided in the tent camps, because they had not had them at their homes in Yemen. However, the larger problem would become having moved in a few hours on the eagles' wings from living in medieval times, to the world of the twentieth century in the technically advanced state of Israel.

There were hundreds of little things that the Yemenites who had lived in southern Arabia for two thousand years had not learned about life in a contemporary modern society. Consider that most of the Yemenites had never seen heavy city automobile traffic, a stop light, a pedestrian crosswalk, or even knew that there were rules of the road. This and a hundred other things were to confront them as they slowly adjusted to their new life in the Promised Land. Everything considered, under the circumstances they handled it well, and quickly earned the respect of the already established Israelis.

Many of the early Jewish Yemenite refugees that had left Yemen illegally, before Iman Ahmad issued the decree that allowed them to leave in May of 1949, arrived in Israel with some in very poor physical condition, and were in need of medical assistance on arrival. Until the medical unit at camp Hashed was established and operating, there was no medical facility in Aden to care for the Yemenite Jewish refugees. In March and April of 1949, when we were making the emergency Yemenite evacuation flights, our Yemenite passengers had had no facilities to bathe, wash the clothes they might be wearing, or receive any medical treatment since they had left Yemen.

By July, when camp Hashed finally opened, the "Magic Carpet" flights were carrying Yemenites that had clothing supplied, medical check-ups, received food and shower baths before the flights, and were much better prepared to travel on the wings' of an Eagle.

The older refugees were the ones that had the hardest time in adjusting to the new environment. Children seemed to adjust much faster, and quickly learned the new ways of doing things.

Thanks to the preparations that the JDC and Israeli government had made earlier, within a few months they were able to react financially, and physically, with the resources to provide housing, medical facilities, schools, and social personnel to aid the thousands of refugees on arrival. Yes, it was hectic and far less than perfect at first, but as the building of transit camps and their facilities caught up with the number of incoming-refugees arriving, things became a lot better.

The more difficult problem was organizing the thousands of new arrivals, and providing them with productive jobs. Most of the skills of the Yemenite refugee workers were in the making of jewelry, tailoring, masonry, carpentry, pottery, blacksmiths, shoe-making, and weaving. While they couldn't immediately put everyone to work in the trades they were trained in, they developed large useful projects that required a lot of unskilled labor with little other associated costs.

Harvesting crops, like picking oranges, was a job that was labor intensive. Some other examples were the planting of millions of trees on the barren hills of the country to bring back the forests that in times past were growing there. Large scale irrigation systems were built to provide water to barren land on which future farming would be developed, and the preparation of underground sewer, water, drainage systems, roads and grading, for sites of future homes, factories, shopping centers, and schools to be built on when needed in the future.

The concept put every able bodied man to work doing something that would one day be of value, and benefit the general economy. As the refugees poured in over the next few years, these sites were developed into towns and business centers much faster than anyone had thought was possible when the plan was designed. It actually enabled Israel to become an economically viable state in a relatively short time.

As the Yemenite children completed their schooling they became part of a motivated, educated, and dedicated work force for Israel's industries, business, and military interests the likes of nothing anyone had ever seen in the Middle-East before.

Now, three generations later, they are a respected historic part of Israel's population. After thousands of years they are at home in the land that was promised to them in Genesis a long, long, long time ago.

After the Yemenites had become somewhat accustomed to life in the 20th Century, they were free to live in Israel or to migrate to anyplace that was available. After they had regained their health, many of the older men were able to find work in the crafts they had learned in Yemen. A very large percentage of the younger men joined the Israeli Military and served a mandatory enlistment period learning the art of modern warfare. They would also receive training in a craft that would be of use to them and the Israeli economy when their enlistment period was over. This would enable them to support themselves in the general economy, but they would also be subject to periodic recalls to military service for training, or in an emergency.

The Yemenite children were enrolled in schools for the first time in their lives, and received a well oriented education as they grew-up and matured in Israel.

Not all of the Yemenites remained in Israel. Many continued their migration to live in the United States, and a few chose to settle in other countries.

Many of those Yemenite immigrants found ways to earn a good education for themselves and their children, and applied the knowledge gained to do very well in the economy. Three generations later their off-spring has merged into the local society, but almost like it was a genetic trait they have not forgotten their Yemenite history, customs, or religion.

Your author was a part of the generation that saw the founding of the State of Israel, and participated in returning the Jewish Yemenite refugees to their Promised Land. As there are few of us remaining, I thought you might like to hear my story before I too join my comrades of 1949 that I shared this wonderful adventure of a lifetime with.

Not often are we as individuals able to directly help tens-of-thousands of people have a better life.

In 2012, I was able to interview a family whose father had flown from Aden to Israel "On Eagles' Wings" in October of 1950. The father's name is Ely Dromy, and he and other members of the family express in a video interview the effect that the flight "On Eagles' Wings" had on their lives.

For further information about this and other books by Elgen Long, go to www.elgenlong.com. Biographical information of Captain Long is available there as well as additional information that might have been obtained after the books have been distributed.

I do hope that descendants and others with additional knowledge of any of the books contents will make contact so it can be distributed to all of our readers, and be available in the future to all interested parties.

And yes, I still often wonder if all of this could have really come-about by pure happenstance.

Chapter Twelve
THE END OF OPERATION MAGIC CARPET

> *Then shall they know that I am the Lord their God,*
> *which caused them to be led into captivity among the heathen:*
> *but I have gathered them unto their own land,*
> *and have left none of them any more there.*
>
> ### *Ezekiel 39:28*

On Monday, March 21, 2016 your author was waiting patiently at his home in Reno, Nevada for the final proof copy of the eleven chapter book "On Eagles' Wings" to be delivered from the printer.

Nearly half-a-world away in Israel an announcement by the Chairman of the Jewish Agency, Natan Sharansky, former Soviet Union human rights protester and chess grand master, revealed that a highly significant moment in the history of Israel had occurred the night before, when the final group of Yemenite Jews had arrived in Israel at Ben Gurion International Airport.

Mr. Sharansky explained, "From Operation Magic Carpet in 1949 to the present day, the Jewish Agency had helped bring Yemenite Jewry home to Israel. Today we bring that historic mission to a close."

Mr. Arielle Di-Porto, also of the Jewish Agency, reported that the last complex and covert operation was given the name "Mikeitze Teiman," a Hebrew phrase taken from Genesis 41:1, loosely translated as, "the end of the Yemen operation." The final flight took months to organize and was planned with assistance from the American State Department.

These announcements of the final flight suggested that adding a twelfth chapter to "On Eagles' Wings" could close the circle of the story of the greatest airlift of refugees of its time. It is a happy conclusion.

The information this author has been able to find indicates that the very first flight made to rescue Yemenite Jews from Aden to Israel was a roundtrip flight made by future El Al Captain and Chief Pilot, Sam Lewis in late December of 1948. However, the specifics of that flight are not recorded so no comparison can be made to the number of refugees flown to Israel then or the type of aircraft used in the subsequent missions.

The rescue of Yemenite Jews had continued since 1950 when "Operation Magic Carpet" supposedly had ended sporadically with the subsequent flights being kept highly secret. Those covert operations brought several hundred Yemenite Jews to Israel especially in the 1980's and 1990's.

The cessation announcement reported that it was a small group of 17 passengers brought to Israel during the final mission of operation "Mikietz Teiman," bringing to an end the 67-year-old "Operation Magic Carpet." The late-Sunday night arrival at Ben Gurion International Airport included a family of five from Sanaa, and the last twelve Jews from the town of Radah, along with their Rabbi who was hand-carrying a 500 year old Torah scroll.

It was also reported that approximately 40 to 50 Yemenite Jews have chosen to remain in Yemen despite the risks of the current political turmoil in that country. Most of them are reported to reside in a walled compound adjacent to the inactive American Embassy in Sanaa under the marginal protection of the Yemeni authorities.

While this was the official end of "Operation Magic Carpet" and an estimated 2,000 years of Jewish presence in Yemen, the Yemenite traditions will live on in Israel.

Since the establishment of the State of Israel in 1948, well over 50,000 Yemenite Jews have immigrated, with nearly 50,000 arriving during 1949 and 1950 on "Operation Magic Carpet" alone. It is estimated that there are now more than 350,000 Yemeni-Israelis living in Israel. Most are descendants of the Yemenite Jews that were flown to Israel during the "On the Eagles' Wings" and "The Magic Carpet" operations in 1949 and 1950.

As far as the author knows, the twelve Alaska Airlines flights referenced in earlier chapters carrying Jewish Yemenite families from Aden to Israel during March and April of 1949 were the only flights made during the secret operation officially called, "On the Eagles' Wings." If Yemeni-Israeli families stories report your ancestors traveling with no seats in the airplane, no seat belts, no food, and passengers packed like sardines, chances are those ancestors were the subject of the foregoing story and the author was intimately involved as the flight navigator. The crew-members mentioned were the only ones that operated the emergency evacuation flights from Aden to Israel carrying the refugees without seats.

It is reasonably assumed that the flights were the first commercial, international airline flights made by aircraft carrying passengers without seats or restraint in a bare cabin without the assistance and safety provided by flight attendants.

This was only done because of the life and death situation the refuges faced at the time. Permission for such configuration would never have been granted by regulatory authorities even if requested, and so it became an early example of it being better to ask for forgiveness than to ask permission. However, the procedure proved so successful in emergency situations that it has been used many times since by El Al, as mentioned earlier in "Operation Solomon." As recently as 2013, the "emergency no-seat" procedure was used by the U.S. Military in the Philippines when evacuating survivors off the Island of Tacloban after it was devastated by Super-Typhoon Haiyan.

The ancestors of Yemeni-Israelis made history in Israel before it was even a year old, and shared with our "ironman" crew the making of aviation history. It was the early refugee flights made by the ancestors and Alaska Airlines that defined the efficient method that was followed by "Operation Magic Carpet" in the airlifting of most Yemeni refugee in 1949 and 1950, and the eventual removal of all but a few of the Jewish population of Yemen to Israel concluding 67 years later on March 21, 2016.

Credit for organizing and facilitating the successful completion of the "Aliyah" of Yemenite Jews must be given to many groups and individuals previously referenced, who collectively financed, planned, and executed the whole operation. The real heroes were the Jewish Yemenites themselves who risked everything to make their "Aliyah" to the land of their prophesies, the newly formed State of Israel.

Of the approximately 51,000 Yemenite Jews, of all ages and physical conditions, the vast majority successfully completed their "Aliyah" to Israel. Of those who were not able to complete their journey, none were lost due to the operations of the Magic Carpet.

Special credit should also be given to the British Forces in The Aden Protectorate during 1949 and 1950. Without much homeland support or fanfare, they were very deeply involved in building Camp Hashed for humane transit accommodations and facilitating the flights from Khormaksar Royal Air Force Station in Aden to the Lydda Airport in Israel. Of course Israel played an important role in providing funds, medical personnel, and staff to prepare and care for the Yemenites prior to their departure to Israel. Once they arrived in Israel the government cared for their needs until they could be integrated independently into the Israeli Society. The Israeli Government was greatly assisted and supported by the independent Jewish Agency.

The American Jewish Joint Distribution Committee, whose members of its executive committee we flew from The Netherlands to Israel on April 9,

1949, supplied guidance and funds to support the operation. The United States Congress provided funds that President of the United States Harry S. Truman approved with gratitude, and The United Nations Security Council and Refugee Program also lent support to the Yemenite Jewish refugees in their desire to migrate to Israel.

To the "ironman" crew and this author it was a distinct honor to have been able to be of service to the Yemenite Jews in helping them complete their Aliyah to Israel "On the Eagles' Wings" and "Operation Magic Carpet."

I believe to all who participated it was an adventure of a lifetime.

Epilogue

As unlikely as it might seem, the following events just happened without any pre-planning or forethought. I know I did not think anything about it at the time, and I can't think of any reason why anyone else should have either. Just happenstance, I guess.

It wasn't long after returning home from flying the Yemenite refugees on "Operation Magic Carpet," that Alaska Airlines was forced by the CAA and CAB government bodies to curtail their international charter operations. With the curtailment of international flights, the need for navigators was reduced, and I received a furlough notice.

In June of 1950, Israel's National Airline, El Al, hired me to navigate their new flight service across the North Atlantic between New York and Tel Aviv. I was based in New York, and had the honor of navigating the second revenue flight El Al made from New York across the Atlantic.

The flight departed Idlewild Airport (now John F. Kennedy), New York, on June 25, 1950 on El Al, DC-4 aircraft 4X-ACC, with Captain Henry "Hank" Mullineaux, and Navigator Elgen Long. It was the second revenue flight El Al had ever made out of New York across the Atlantic.

We returned from Shannon, Ireland to New York on June 27, 1950 flying the El Al, DC-4 aircraft 4X-ADC. This marked the start of weekly DC-4 charter service by El Al between Israel and New York. During the month of July, 1950 I made two more round trips across the Atlantic from New York to Europe with Captain Mullineaux.

On August 14, 1950 I made a trip as navigator from New York to Shannon, Ireland with Captain Robert F. "Bob" Maguire in El Al, DC-4 aircraft 4X-ADC. This may have been one of the last trips Captain Maguire flew, as I know sometime there after he lost his Civil Aeronautics Administration pilot's medical certificate due to a heart condition.

On August 17, 1950 I returned from Shannon to New York with Captain Sam Lewis on El Al, DC-4 aircraft 4X-ADC. From August 17th through September 11th I would fly three more trips across the Atlantic with Captain Sam Lewis.

To the best of my memory, in 1950, Bob Maguire was V.P. of Operations for El Al in New York, and Sam Lewis was Chief pilot for El Al in London.

In June of 1949, Bob Maguire had been Vice-President of Operations for Near East Air Transport, and Hank Mullineaux was the Chief Pilot during the start of "Operation Magic Carpet." Sam Lewis was reported to have made the first or one of the very earliest, Jewish Yemenite refugee flights from Aden to Lydda on December 28, 1948.

These three men were all heavily involved in the organization and initial operations of the greatest air rescue operation in history. They were the men that put "Operation Magic Carpet" into operation, and got the diverse group of planes and flight crews into the air.

During June, July, August, and September of 1950, I flew with these three men, split many beers, had many meals, and spent hundreds of hours in the same cockpit during flights with them, and never once did any of us broach the subject of flying the Jewish Yemenites from Aden to Lydda. Perhaps it was because of the veil of secrecy that the flights were still under, that prevented us from discussing probably the most important thing we had ever done. More likely, as I seem to recollect those events, none of us yet realized the value and importance of what we had accomplished with those flights.

We were paid for the flights, and it was our job to do the best we could in flying them, but just like during WW II at the time, we seldom knew the importance of our mission or the benefits that millions of people might harvest from it. Many years would have to pass before we would come to realize the full-impact and value of what had been accomplished.

I received notice that I was being called back from furlough by the Flying Tiger Line, and would be based in Burbank, California. I gave notice to El Al that I was resigning my navigator's position with them at their New York base, and returned to Los Angeles and the Flying Tiger Line.

I accomplished three things over the next two years. I flew as a navigator full time with the Flying Tigers, built a new home for my wife and two children, and during periods of free time completed my flight training and was certificated by the CAA to be an airline co-pilot.

In March of 1952, I was hired by the Flying Tiger Line as a co-pilot, and assigned to fly Curtiss C-46 aircraft on their domestic air-freight flights between Burbank, California and Denver, Colorado. In 1957, I received my FAA Airline Transport Rating, and was promoted to Captain by the Flying Tiger Line.

Most of my future flying was to be with the Flying Tiger Line. It was to be an exciting and rewarding forty-year career in aviation that would take another book or two to tell about. Maybe someday I'll get to it, but in the meantime I'll post a short biographical sketch you can look at if you would like.

Over the years quite a lot has happened, and somehow I've always been extremely lucky. I hold many flying records and firsts, but I am proudest of the Institute of Navigation award as the world's outstanding practicing navigator, and the Federation Aeronautic International "Gold Air Medal" as the outstanding sport pilot in the world for 1971. Those are the world's two highest awards in two separate categories of aviation expertise.

On August 12, 1987, I retired at age 60 from the Flying Tiger Line, as No. 1 Captain on the Flying Tiger Line Pilots Seniority List, Senior Boeing-747 Pilot, and Senior Captain on the Flying Tiger Line's Pilot's Revue Board. After 45 years and some 45,000 hours of time in the air, I was lucky enough to have never had an aircraft accident or have been issued a violation.

See what I mean about my suspicions of happenstance. Go figure; how could all of this just have happened to this small-town boy from the Oregon Coast.

A brief sketch of my career follows.

CAPTAIN ELGEN M. LONG, FTL [RET.]

BIOGRAPHICAL SKETCH: Elgen M. Long was born August 12, 1927 in McMinnville, Oregon. He married Marie K. Kurilich on May 12, 1946 in Los Angeles, California. They had two children, Donna Marie and Harry Elgen Long. After 57 years together, Marie passed away June 20, 2003. On January 17, 2011, Elgen Long married Kay N. Otto at Incline Village, Lake Tahoe, Nevada.

AWARDS AND ACCOMPLISHMENTS: Winner FAI "Gold Air Medal" Outstanding Sports Pilot in the World; The Institute of Navigation "Superior Achievement Award" as practicing Navigator; Airline Pilots Association "Award for Outstanding Airmanship"; "Franklin Harris Trophy" for first solo flight around-the-world over both Poles; NAA 2004 "Crystal Eagle Award" for Lifetime Achievement in Aviation; Holder of 15 aviation World Records and Firsts. 2009, FAA, The Wright Brothers "Master Pilot" award for fifty years of dedicated service in Aviation Safety. In 2012, Captain Elgen M. Long was inducted by the Oregon State Board of Aviation into the "Oregon Aviation Hall of Honor."

EDUCATION: Graduate, Marshfield High School (GED 1946) Coos Bay, Oregon. U.S. Navy 1942-1946. Attended Aviation Radio School, Aerial Gunnery School, Advanced Aviation Radio School, Radar Bombing, and Aerial Navigation School. Elgen received an AA degree in Aeronautics, from the College of San Mateo, California, and studied Aircraft Accident Investigation at the University of Southern California and the Norton AFB Crash Laboratory.

APPOINTMENTS: Airline Pilot Accident Investigator 1957; U. S. Department of Transportation Accident Prevention Counselor 1971; Senior Captain B-747, Pilots Review Board FTL 1987; Accompanied former FAA Administrator, Admiral Donald Engen, as Flight Training Specialist for his 1988 Peoples Republic of China Tour and Airline Safety Review. Expedition Leader 2002 Earhart Aircraft search mission, WID Search Advisor during 2006, and 2009 Catalyst II missions.

CAREER: 1942-46 Over 100 U.S. Navy combat missions in seaplanes during World War II as Radioman and Navigator, including Howland Island patrols where Amelia Earhart disappeared.

1947-1987 I was a Radioman, Navigator, Captain, Instructor, and Check-Pilot for Flying Tiger Line. A 70 year flying career that totaled nearly 45,000 hours of flight without accident or violation. In 1970, I and my wife, Marie, began a 40-year investigation of Amelia Earhart's disappearance at Howland Island.

LICENSES: (FAA) Airline Transport Pilot, Flight Navigator, Flight Radio Operator, Aircraft Power Plant Mechanic.; (FCC) Radio Telegraph Operator with Aeronautical Endorsement, Extra- Class Radio Amateur license W7FT; (British Board of Trade) Air Transport Pilots License.

PROFESSIONAL ASSOCIATIONS: International Society of Air Safety Investigators; Marine Technology Society; American Radio Relay League; National Aeronautics Assoc.; Air Line Pilots Assoc. (ret.); American Polar Society; Old Antarctic Explorers Assoc.; "Fellow National" member of the Explorers Club.

PAST: After 40 years of interviewing over 100 witnesses, examining nearly 25,000 pages of documents, reports, and 2,000 photographs, no credible evidence has been found to change the Navy's 1937 conclusion: Her fuel exhausted, Earhart was forced to ditch her plane into the sea near Howland Island. Elgen and Marie's book, "Amelia Earhart: The Mystery Solved," summarizes the findings and is published by Simon and Schuster. Visit Elgen Long's website at www.ElgenLong.com for more information about his career. Visit www.ElgenLongbooks.com for information on his available books, and the Ely Dromy Family video interview about "The Magic Carpet."

PRESENT: Missions are being planned for an underwater search in the waters near Howland Island where Earhart's missing plane is lying on the ocean floor waiting to be discovered.

FUTURE: When Earhart's Lockheed Electra is found, unmanned vehicles will accomplish a careful forensic analysis of the site before recovery of the plane is made. After recovery, Earhart's plane will be restored and displayed as an artifact of our American heritage.

Photos of author
Captain Elgen M. Long (ret.)

U. S. Navy, 1942.

Boeing 747 Captain, 1978.

Hall of Honor, 2012.

Acknowledgements

Beside my personal logbook, the gathering of much of the information contained in this book was aided by many people in many ways. I must acknowledge and thank them for the unselfish help that they provided.

Penny Brock, friend and neighbor, was the first to suggest that the early Alaska Airline's flights I made in 1949 should be chronicled as she believed they were of great historical value.

Leslie Fried, Curator of the Alaska Jewish Museum in Anchorage for first featuring the early flights of Alaska Airlines by Captain Sam Royal and myself during their grand opening in 2013.

Captain Richard D. Manning USCG Ret., whose constant encouragement and editing-skills helped me keep the writing process moving forward in something like an orderly manner.

Erica Alsberg, former EL AL Flight Attendant and her husband Flying Tiger Line Captain Garry Duff, who helped keep the story on an accurate path without the use of offensive ideas and terms.

Giacinta Bradley Koontz, a friend and author who researched the find of Mr. Ely Dromy. Mr. Dromy, a living Yemenite Refugee that flew on the Magic Carpet, was able to make a video-interview.

To the Ely Dromy Family for the video interview that tells the story of their coming to Israel on the Magic Carpet in the summer of 1950, and the life-changing effect it had on all their lives.

Darragh Metzger, daughter of Captain Warren Metzger, for sharing her memories, copies of her father's log books, and copies of interviews with other associates of early Alaska Airlines.

Retired Los Angeles Sheriff, Michael Poirier, investigator-extraordinaire who came up with innumerable facts and details of people, places, and things that helped keep the book accurate.

To Flying Tiger Line Captain Al Silver, for relating his experiences while flying The Magic Carpet refugees with Flying Tiger Line aircraft that were leased to Near East Air Transport during 1950.

Former Flying Tiger Operations Manager and British RAF veteran, John Townes, whose knowledge of British History and the RAF gave us a great advantage in completing the research.

British Archivist, Liz Sutherland, who with knowledge and determination, finally found the 1949 RAF reports from Khormaksar RAF Station that we needed to accurately complete the story.

British RAF photographer Keith James, who shared the pictures and memories he possessed of Khormaksar RAF Station while we were making the Yemenite Refugee rescue flights.

To Sandra Fruechting, and her brother Rabbi Steve Stern who provided us with his valuable perspective and advice along with the thoughtful recommendations of two Israeli Historians.

Sigrid Powell, designer and artist, whose patience and talent helped put this book together in a coherent and readable manner in a subtle and effective style.

And last but not least, to my wife Kay, who continuously kept the home fires burning while I was off in my office for months on end, devoting most of my attention to writing this book.

For anyone I inadvertently left out here, I really meant to thank you too. I ask your pardon, until we meet again so I can thank you in person.